THE WAR ON CA$H

How Banks and a Power-Hungry Government Want
to Confiscate Your Cash, Steal Your Liberty and
Track Every Dollar You Spend
And How to Fight Back

DAVID McREE

Humanix Books

www.humanixbooks.com

Humanix Books

The War on Cash
Copyright © 2020 by David McRee
All rights reserved

Humanix Books, P.O. Box 20989, West Palm Beach, FL 33416, USA
www.humanixbooks.com | info@humanixbooks.com

Humanix Books is a division of Humanix Publishing, LLC. Its trademark, consisting of the words "Humanix Books" is registered in the Patent and Trademark Office and in other countries.

Disclaimer: The information presented in this book is meant to be used for general resource purposes only; it is not intended as specific financial advice for any individual and should not substitute financial advice from a finance professional.

ISBN: 9781630061531 (Trade Paper)
ISBN: 9781630061548 (E-book)

Printed in the United States of America

CONTENTS

PREFACE

POWERFUL FORCES ARE AT work, and they are not working for your personal benefit. All over the world, including in the United States of America, governments, certain academics, banks and civil service organizations (including large non-governmental organizations [NGOs]) are cooperating to stop you from using cash.

They want you to have no option but to pay for everything you buy using electronic payment systems. They want you to be unable to go to a bank and withdraw your money in cash. They want you to be afraid to have more than a few dollars cash on your person, in your home, or in your car.

Laws have already been passed in Europe and the United States to restrict the use of cash for certain things. Banks are adopting policies against keeping cash in a safe deposit box, or paying bills with cash.

Legitimate businesses and their employees are being cut off from the banking system because their customers usually pay in cash, or because the businesses sell a legal product or service that the government does not approve of.

The IRS has seized bank accounts of people and businesses that have done nothing wrong except make regular deposits of less than $10,000 to their bank account.

Law enforcement officers are seizing cash from anyone they think is carrying too much cash. If you have more than a couple of hundred bucks on you, you're suspected of being a drug dealer or a terrorist. No drugs or bombs need be in your possession. The cash is the evidence.

In this book I have five goals:

1. To show you that the outrageous attacks on your natural rights as mentioned above are actually happening.

2. To convince you that the use and possession of cash is essential to a free and prosperous society.

3. To show you that these attacks on your cash and your privacy are not isolated events, but are representative of a worldwide trend that is affecting everyone and involves mega-millions of dollars.

4. To show you that unless something is done, there is a high likelihood that you will lose the ability to meaningfully use cash in your lifetime or you will be persecuted for your use of cash.

5. And finally, to suggest how you can fight back.

When I first conceived of the idea and title for this book, I had actually not heard the phrase "war on cash" used in the media. But within a few weeks of beginning my outline, libertarian and conservative websites began using the phrase. "Cashless economy" and "cashless society" are other terms often used instead of "war on cash" and are often found in articles that stress the convenience aspect of electronic transactions and the inconvenience of cash. But there is much more to a cashless society than the aspect of convenience. It finds its dark heart in a government's fundamental distrust of its citizens.

Although the coordinated actions that create the modern war on cash are fairly recent, the idea of a cashless society isn't. As far back as the 1960's ". . . it was widely predicted that electronic fund transfer [EFT] . . . would replace checks and even cash as the primary method for exchanging value in the United States." Of course, this did not come to pass quickly, because consumers were not particularly interested in electronic transactions. Nevertheless, banks pushed forward with EFT systems to reduce the expense of handling huge volumes of checks and to reduce the number of people needed to process them, including bank tellers.[1] The genesis of the movement toward a cashless society began as a cost-saving measure for financial institutions. It has evolved into a coordinated effort by governments, financial institutions, private foundations, NGOs and elite academics to declare war on cash as a means of exchange among people.

What exactly do I mean by "the war on cash?"

The war on cash is the effort by governments around the world to stop people from using cash to pay for things they buy. They do this by making the use of cash suspicious, by passing laws and regulations restricting the use of cash, and by requiring financial institutions to report certain types of cash transactions. The government cannot wage an effective war on cash by itself. It must recruit banks to be its eyes and ears and to put policies in place to make it hard or risky to do business in cash.

The war on cash is not being driven solely by governments. The huge payment processing companies understand that getting a piece of every financial transaction in the world is worth trillions of dollars, and the early bird gets the worm. The data collection industry is also salivating over the profit potential of massive data collection, analysis and sales.

This book is intended to be a wake-up call to anyone not familiar with the tactics being used by governments and their allies to restrict the public's use of cash, and to abuse the laws for their own purposes. It is not intended to be a scholarly or comprehensive work.

People don't need a PhD in meteorology to know when it's raining. All they have to do is open their eyes. Likewise, people don't need a PhD in economics or finance to know when they are being taken advantage of by governments and financial institutions: they just need to open their eyes. This book is intended to be an eye-opener. It covers many angles and provides both an overview for readers new to the topic and a starting point for those doing independent research.

I have provided citations for many of the statements I make in this book to allow readers to verify my sources and to learn more about topics that interest them. I have tried to use sources that are trusted and respected, and I've tried scrupulously to avoid propagandistic articles and websites. In all cases, even though I may only list one citation, I have checked that source against several others. I generally cite the source that I believe to be the most relevant, trustworthy, and complete. In many cases, an article appears on one website and is then echoed all over the web. It can sometimes be difficult to track down the original source. If I could not find a reputable source for a story, I didn't include the information in this book. In some cases, the original internet source is access-limited by a pay wall. In such cases, I have cited another source that summarized or quoted the original, if I found such a source.

Although most of my sources are popular media articles, reports and websites, I cited journal articles if I thought they were relevant. Since this book is written for the layperson, I prefer to use sources that are written for that audience rather than for academics. I do not believe that this in any way detracts from the accuracy or legitimacy of the material I present.

I have made every effort to keep this work from being political. Trying to lay blame on a political party is a distraction that does not serve us. Nevertheless, the competition between the philosophies of collectivism and individual liberty cannot always be ignored or denied.

This book is not an argument against banks, financial institutions or electronic payment systems in general. Not being able to keep your cash in a bank safe is just as bad as not being able to have cash. Without banks of some type we would constantly be targets of robberies and would have to expend a great deal of time and money to defend our money against thieves. Poor countries today, like Haiti, or people unbanked in the United States must expend time, energy and money in an effort to safeguard their cash from thieves, loss, or destruction. Neither eliminating banks nor eliminating cash is the answer.

Although in this book I heap large amounts of criticism on the IRS, it is not a personal attack on individual employees at the IRS. As a CPA, I deal with certain divisions of the IRS on a weekly basis. The IRS has many employees who are fine people and do their best to help, although their hands are tied by the system that has been put in place by politicians and perpetuated by career bureaucrats. Unfortunately, like any large organization, the IRS has its share of sociopathic personalities. All systems eventually benefit from criticisms, so if you're a government employee, don't take it personally. Continue to do what you can from the inside to help people when you can, and blow the whistle when necessary against abuses of power.

As a final note, when I first set out to write this book, I did not fully realize how quickly the war on cash was escalating. Almost every day I find new developments and headlines on the news sources I follow. My hope is that the evidence I present will be persuasive, and that the consequences of abolishing cash will be seen for what they are: unacceptable.

INTRODUCTION

THERE'S SOMETHING MAGICAL ABOUT the sight of cash and coin. It attracts the eye. Even the sight of one shiny dime on the sidewalk will cause most people to stoop to pick it up. But as much as we love cash, most of us don't have a clue about what it represents and why it exists, and we often confuse the concept of money with cash. They are not always the same thing.

Governments hate cash. Let me qualify that statement: governments hate cash when it's in your hands. Government officials love cash when it's in their hands. And so they are adding yet another war to their endless string of wars: a war on cash. Your cash.

Governments are in the counterfeiting business on a scale not even dreamed of by the common criminal or by the Mafia. But even that isn't enough. They want your cash. All of it. Because it's hard to control and monitor money when it is in the form of cash in your pocket. They are busy passing laws to make it hard for you to have cash and to use cash.

Making regular cash deposits can turn you into a criminal suspect and result in your bank account being confiscated by the government. Making regular cash withdrawals from your bank account can have the same result. Carrying large amounts of cash on your person can lead to your cash being seized without your even being charged with a crime. As you'll see shortly, even carrying as little as $2,400 cash in your car while you're on vacation can result in seizure by law enforcement. And buying a car with cash of more than $10,000 from a car dealer will result in your identity being checked against a list of known terrorists and the transaction will be reported to the government.

The government does everything it can to track every dollar you earn and spend. It requires banks to report certain cash deposits and transactions. It requires certain businesses that pay you for services to report those payments to the IRS on Form 1099 — forced snitching, if you will.

If the government can eliminate cash from the system, it can control everything you do. Ever heard of Operation Chokepoint? This is where the government decides that it doesn't like you or your legitimate business and forces your bank to close your accounts. If your business depends on customers who pay with checks, debit cards, or credit cards, you are out of business without access to a bank account and payment processors.

The whole time it's making war on your hard-earned cash, it's deliberately, knowingly, and brazenly devaluing your money every day by creating inflation. Do you know what inflation is? Inflation is when those greedy capitalists keep raising prices so they can keep growing their overstuffed bank accounts, right? Wrong. If you already know what inflation really is, you're among an elite few. Everyone needs to understand that inflation doesn't just happen: it is created by the government. More about that later.

Let's get on with it.

CHAPTER 1

Money and Cash

———————————

MONEY CAN TAKE MANY FORMS. It could be gold or silver, paper or shells. Even stolen Tide laundry detergent is being used as money in some of the inner city black markets, mostly to use in payment for drugs.[1.1] Honeybuns are used as money in some prisons.[1.2] For the most part, today's money is in the form of checks and check cards, credit (debt), and various forms of electronic currency transfers. Cash is nothing more than the physical manifestation of money.

If a check is lost in the mail, it can be replaced and nothing is lost. If a $100 bill gets lost in the mail, it is simply gone. That's the risk and the beauty of cash: it's anonymous. It's largely untraceable in its current form. Cash is always considered money, but money takes many forms other than cash.

Bitcoin is a new form of money that many people are excited about, but it is not cash.

How much money is there in the United States, and how much of it is physical cash? According to the Federal Reserve, "There was approximately $1.70 trillion in circulation as of January 31, 2019. This figure includes Federal Reserve notes ($1,655.2 billion), U.S. notes ($0.2 billion), currency no longer issued ($0.2 billion), and coins outstanding ($47.2 billion)."[1.3] The key here is "in circulation." Currency in circulation refers to U.S. coins and paper currency in the hands of the public. That means it's not in the bank: it's in your wallet, in a cash register, under your mattress, or buried in your back yard.

According to the New York Federal Reserve Board's web site: ". . . as much as two-thirds of U.S. currency in circulation may be held outside the United States . . ." But even though it is not present in the country, it is still counted in the money supply, because it can be spent on goods and services in the U.S. economy.[1.4] Here's another interesting fact: the most popular denomination of Federal Reserve note outside of the United States is the $100 bill. That's right. There are more $100 bills outside the U.S. than inside. But then you probably already knew that just by looking in your wallet. Many of those foreign-located $100 bills are held by central banks, drug cartels, and perhaps oil sheiks.

So, let's do a little calculation. Don't worry: I'll do all the math. Since there is about $1,700,000,000,000 (that's $1.7 trillion) of cash in circulation and only one third of that is held in wallets inside the United States, that means about $566,666,666,667 ($566.7 billion) is in circulation inside the U.S.; since there are roughly 253,000,000 adults in the U.S. in 2018, we can say that there is enough cash in circulation for each U.S. resident adult to have about $2,240 dollars in their pockets or under their mattress.[1.5] Do you have your share?

Although it's easy to learn how much cash is in circulation, it's not as easy to figure out how much money in U.S. dollars exists in the world. It's like trying to answer the question: "How many doves are resting on tree branches in the world right now?" It's

unanswerable. Various sources put the number around $10 tril-
lion. And, also according to "various sources," about 90 percent of
that $10 trillion is electronic money. In other words, it's not cash
and never will be turned into cash. You can't see it or touch it. It
exists only as digital bits on a computer in a central bank, created
by monetary magic possessed only by the bank.

CHAPTER 2

Race to a
Cashless Economy

CASH FRUSTRATES GOVERNMENTS. It's too hard to trace, and governments the world over want to know how much money you earn, how much money you have, and what you buy with your money. They want to make sure they get their "fair" share of your earnings and of your wealth. The ideal monetary system from a government's perspective is a cashless system where all of your transactions are electronic and therefore traceable directly to you. Because the government does not trust you, it cannot trust you either to remit your "fair share" of taxes or spend your money on the things it thinks are in your best interest.

Cash is also a problem for banks, which we'll get into shortly. When governments and banks have problems, they turn to academics to help them craft a solution. That's where the economists get involved. There are some very influential economists getting behind the movement to eliminate the cash from your wallet.

As I write this, governments and financial institutions in the U.S. and around the world are working harder than ever to eliminate cash. In some cases they want to criminalize cash and are making great progress in that regard, but eliminating it entirely by fiat may prove to be beyond the reach of most governments. It will be a lot easier just to intimidate people into shunning cash. Nevertheless, quite a few countries conduct the majority of consumer-to-business transactions without using cash. A quick internet search in 2015 turned up the following headlines (among many others) from 2012 through 2015 on the first few pages of internet search results:

- Nordic Countries Point the Way to Cashless Societies — Reuters

- A Shift Toward Digital Currency — *New York Times*

- The Slow Death of Cash — MIT Technology Review

- Sweden May be First Country to Eliminate Cash — geek.com

- Will Israel be the World's First 'No Cash' State? — Israelnationalnews.com

- The Case to Get Rid of Paper Money — fortune.com

- The Benefits of Getting Rid of Cash — economist.com

- The Hubris of Trying to Eliminate Cash — theatlantic.com

By January 2020, it was obvious from the internet search results below that several countries have made considerable progress toward becoming cashless since about 2013, with Sweden taking the lead. Consider this collection of articles from 2018 and 2019:

- Which Country Will Be the First Cashless Country in the World? — Nayax.com (a fintech company)

- The 10 Most Cashless Countries in the World — telegraph.co.uk

- Could These Countries Be Cash-Free by 2020?
  — medium.com

- Going Cashless: What Can We Learn from Sweden's Experience? — knowledge.wharton.upenn.edu

- Rich Countries Must Start Planning for a Cashless Future — economist.com

- Sweden's Cashless Experiment: Is It Too Much Too Fast? — NPR.org

- Visa Sets Sights on a "Cashless Japan" — usa.visa.com

In 2015, the Swedish central bank projected that the amount of cash in Sweden would fall by 20 to 50 percent between 2012 and 2020.[2.1] A 2018 Riksbank annual survey of payment patterns in Sweden revealed that "80 percent of the survey respondents said they used a debit card for their most recent purchase. The corresponding figure for 2016 was 64%." The number of survey respondents reporting that they had used cash for their most recent purchase has been declining by about 15 percent each year on average, and over time fewer respondents expressed negative feelings about the declining opportunities to use cash.[2.2]

Why is what's happening in Sweden and other early adopters of cash-free economies important? It's because these countries are proving grounds. When the bugs are worked out in these forward-leaning countries, the "solutions" will quickly spread around the world. Success in these countries will give banks, governments, and fintech companies the experience and confidence they need to push "cashlessness" onto more reluctant populations. It is also important to watch these early-adopters to observe the problems they encounter that don't have satisfactory tech solutions, causing the cashless cartel to resort to psychological operations on large populations to persuade them to abandon cash, or to place restrictive limits and fees on people who continue to use cash.

NPR's All Things Considered program reported in 2019 that in Sweden "another concern is that the majority of local bank branches have stopped letting people take out cash or even bring cash into the bank."

Swedish professor Niklas Arvidsson and Riksbank researcher Björn Segendorf have predicted that by 2023, cash may no longer be a generally accepted way of paying in Sweden.[2.3]

German DW-TV reporter Hanspeter Michel reports on a woman operating a gas station at a Swedish marina who still accepts cash as a courtesy to her customers, but that she cannot wait until cash disappears. Why? The banks in her area no longer accept cash deposits, so she has to make 30-minute trips to a special location each week to deposit cash from her business. She has to pay 20 Euros for each bag of cash and coin she deposits. To take out cash from the bank to make change for her customers, she has to pay a bank fee of nearly 200 Euros, which is often more than the amount of change she needs to withdraw.[2.4]

This cashless society concept is being promoted as more convenient and more secure for consumers. although with all the credit card fraud and identity theft these days, it's hard to imagine that anyone believes a cashless society is more secure. Countries with some of the highest tax rates are the ones most interested in going cashless. CNBC reported in late 2014 that the following countries have made the greatest progress toward cashless societies expressed as a percentage of the total value of consumer payments.[2.5]

- South Korea: 70 percent of consumer transactions are non-cash.
- Germany: 76 percent non-cash.
- U.S.A. 80 percent non-cash.
- The Netherlands: 85 percent non-cash.
- Australia: 86 percent non-cash.

- Sweden: 89 percent non-cash.

- United Kingdom: 89 percent non-cash.

- Canada: 90 percent non-cash.

- France: 92 percent non-cash.

The percentage of non-cash transactions around the world varies according to who's doing the reporting and whether the percentage is of total transactions or of consumer transactions, but the clear trend is toward an increase in non-cash transactions. In 2019, just 2 percent of the total value of transactions in Sweden consist of cash, and that's expected to drop to less than half a percent by 2020.[2.6]

Many European countries now prohibit cash transactions above a certain amount. Payments above that threshold amount must be made by bank transfer, checks, or credit/debit card.

France limits a resident's consumer cash transactions to 1,000 Euros as of September 2015. This applies to transactions between consumers and businesses, not between private individuals.[2.7]

In Spain, the limit is 2,500 Euros.

In Italy, cash transactions are limited to 2,999.99 Euros. Any payment for the rental of real estate cannot be made in cash, regardless of the amount, including vacation rentals.

Greece limits cash payments to 1,500 Euros.[2.8, 2.9]

Of interest, Sweden currently has no limits on cash transactions. I guess they figure if you can find a merchant who will accept cash, spend all you want!

In March 2015 Reuters came out with this bit of news:

"From September [2015] onwards, people who live in France will not be allowed to make payments of more than 1,000 euros ($1,060) in cash, down from 3,000 now. The cap for foreign visitors, left higher for reasons that include facilitating tourism, will be cut to 10,000 euros from 15,000. Any cash deposit or withdrawal of more than 10,000 euros over a single month will be automatically signaled to the Tracfin anti-fraud and money laundering agency.

The authorities will have to be notified over transfers of more than 10,000 euros — for instance cheques, pre-paid cards or gold — by freight within the European Union. Someone changing more than 1,000 euros in cash into another currency will have to show an identity card, down from a previous threshold of 8,000 euros. The government will also increase controls on pre-paid cards and add mini-bank accounts to a national banking database."[2.10]

France is making this move under the guise of fighting terrorism. Terrorists use cash. Get rid of cash — get rid of terrorists.[2.11] Should work, right? Terrorists also use cars and public transportation. They wear shoes and clothes and use cell phones. Should we get rid of those things as well? Joseph Salerno of the Mises Institute observes that a "naked, barefoot terrorist without communications is surely less effective than a fully clothed and equipped one.[2.12]

But these restrictions on using cash will never happen here in the United States, right? Land of the Free, home of the Brave. We'd never put up with that. Don't be so sure. The demonization of cash has been going on a long time. Even local governments resort to restrictions on the use of cash in an effort to combat certain criminal activity.

On July 1, 2011, Louisiana Governor Bobby Jindal signed into law Louisiana Act 389 banning the use of cash by dealers in second-hand "junk."[2.13] The intent of the law was, of course, to make it harder for crooks to deal in stolen merchandise. This law has been widely criticized and even merited a (perhaps sensationalized) mention in Forbes magazine. Let's look at what the law actually does and whom it affects. (Hint: it's not the rich.)

First, the bill defines the people that the law applies to as "secondhand dealers" and describes them this way: "Every person in this state [Louisiana] engaged in the business of buying, selling, trading in, or otherwise acquiring or disposing of junk or used or secondhand property." And "anyone, other than a nonprofit entity, who buys, sells, trades in, or otherwise acquires or disposes of junk or used or secondhand property more frequently than once per month from any other person, other than a nonprofit entity, shall be deemed as being engaged in the business of a secondhand dealer."

The law then goes on to list the type of property you cannot sell for cash to such a secondhand dealer: jewelry, silverware, diamonds, precious metals . . . catalytic converters, auto hulks, copper wire, aluminum other than cans . . . furniture, pictures, objects of art, clothing, mechanic's tools, carpenter's tools, automobile hubcaps, automotive batteries, automotive sound equipment, CB radios, stereos . . . used building components, and many more.

Apparently the law does not prevent the average consumer from walking into a second-hand store and paying cash for a used item. It only applies to prevent the dealer from purchasing items for re-sale using cash.

Chip Cantrell, CPA, provides some interesting commentary on the Louisiana law on his website.[2.14] Cantrell notes that there are some important exceptions in the law. The "no-cash" law does not apply to "nonprofit entities, operations owned by state or local governments, used car operations, auto junk yard dealers, [or to] dealers at gun and knife and other hobby shows." It does not apply to yard sales/garage sales as long as they are not held more often than once per month.

As an example of whom the law will affect, Cantrell mentions a local store where his son likes to purchase video games. In addition to selling new games and game consoles, the store also repurchases used products from their customers to refurbish and re-sell. This game store would be considered a secondhand dealer and would be subject to the new law. Also, people who buy items on Craigslist, EBay, or garage sales for resale would theoretically not be able to use cash for those purchases. As you can see, it affects a lot of small businesses by eliminating their ability to pay cash when purchasing used merchandise. Many dealers in junk are poor and don't have bank accounts. They depend on cash. Receiving a check means paying high fees to cash the checks.

In addition, an entirely new layer of surveillance paperwork is required. The dealer has to get the following information from any seller of used or junk property: name and address, date and place of purchase, driver's license number or other ID number, a photograph of the seller or his or her thumbprints, seller's vehicle license plate number, description of goods purchased from seller, and the seller has to sign a statement that the goods were obtained legally and that they have the right to sell them.

Those records have to be made available to law enforcement for three years. Consequences of failing to make reports available to law enforcement are dire and could involve jail time. Consequences of repeatedly violating certain aspects of the law can result in prison "with or without hard labor." It's in the law.

Attorney Thad D. Ackel, Jr. writes that this " legislation amounts to a public taking of private property without compensation" and that Louisiana's legislators "have effectively banned its citizens from freely using United States legal tender." Further, Ackel observes: "Regardless of whether or not the transaction information is connected with, or law enforcement is investigating a crime, individuals and businesses are forced to report routine business activity to the police."[2.15]

Is this massive inconvenience and invasion of privacy necessary to nab a few people who deal in stolen property? Is there not a better way? And how long before these types of laws expand to cover all transactions? When has any law remained confined to its original scope?

Banks are boldly working in cooperation with and often at the behest of the government in the process of eliminating cash.

JPMorgan Chase bank has tightened the noose on people who prefer to use cash for all of their transactions. Chase has rolled out a new policy in selected US markets that ". . . restricts borrowers from using cash to make payments on credit cards, mortgages, equity lines, and auto loans." The January 2019 Safe Deposit Lease Agreement at Chase Bank provides that "You agree not to use the box to store money, coin or currency unless it is of a collectable nature . . ."[2.16] Can you imagine that? You can't put your cash in a safe deposit box?[2.17] Doesn't that make you a bit uncomfortable?

In a related posting to the Mises Institute's Facebook page, Joseph Salerno writes:[2.18]

"It is hardly surprising that a crony capitalist fractional-reserve bank, which received $25 billion in bailout loans from the U.S. Treasury, should want to curry favor with its regulators and political masters and, in the process, ensure its own stability by helping to stamp out the use of cash. For the very existence of cash places the power over fractional-reserve banks squarely in the hands of their depositors who may withdraw their cash in any amount and at any time, bringing even the mightiest bank to its knees literally overnight (e.g., Washington Mutual). What is surprising is how little notice the rollout of Chase's new policy has received."

Kiplinger advises that ". . . some banks expressly forbid storing cash in a safe deposit box. Read the fine print of your agreement."[2.19]

Not satisfied with the speed at which businesses are adopting a cashless business model, in 2017 Visa announced ". . . The Visa Cashless Challenge, with a call to action for small business restaurants, cafes, or food truck owners to describe what cashless means for them, their employees and customers. Visa will be awarding up to $500,000 to 50 eligible US-based small business food service owners who commit to joining the 100% cashless quest."[2.20] Each business that opts in to the program will receive $10,000 to help their transition to a cashless payments system.[2.21]

In an effort to jump-start a lagging economy and fight tax-evasion, the Prime Minister of Greece is forcing Greek citizens to spend 30% of their income electronically. Failure to do so will result in a 22% tax on the shortfall. The Greek government expects to raise 500 million Euros each year with these penalty taxes. The banks will report each person's spending to the government to facilitate enforcement.[2.22]

Governments, in cooperation with banks, can and will eliminate the use of cash as they see fit. Even in the United States.

In pursuit of greater profits, it is obviously in the interest of banks, payment processors and financial technology companies to decrease the use of cash and increase the use of digital payment systems. In an opinion piece for *The Guardian*, Brett Scott observes that by shutting down branches and ATMs, banks make it harder and harder for people to use cash. People then have no choice but to increase their use of digital payments, which then allows the banks to say they are closing branches and ATMs because fewer people are using them. It isn't that cash is less convenient. It's that banks are making cash less convenient. This is how banks and other powerful entities "nudge" people toward the preferred behavior.[2.23]

It has not escaped notice that outlawing the use of cash is unconstitutional on its face. However a frequent retort is: "Since when does the government care about the Constitution?" The people may have the Constitution, but the government has the perpetually campaigning legislature, the largely rubber-stamp judiciary, the monarchist executive branch, and the guns and prisons. Let's not forget the guns and prisons.

CHAPTER 3

War on Cash — First Shots Fired

BACK IN THE 1980'S, I made my living doing lawn maintenance and landscaping. One customer owned a tire store and auto repair shop. He was at least 30 years older than I, and his tire shop was very successful, even though its modest appearance would not give that away. Often, as I was finishing up his lawn at his residence late in the afternoon, he'd drive up in an old car (with brand new tires). He always said hello and asked if his wife had paid me yet. If I said she hadn't, he'd pull out his wallet, stuffed with cash, and dig out some bills. One day he said, "David, have you ever seen a thousand-dollar bill?" Of course, I answered "No!" I don't think I'd seen a thousand dollars cash in one place in any denomination. He dug into his wallet and extracted a $1,000 bill. Showing it to me he said, "They don't make them anymore. Thought you'd like to see one before they disappear. I carry it around as a conversation piece." We both laughed, but I laughed in amazement that someone driving a 15-year old faded blue car would carry around a thousand-dollar bill as a conversation piece. That's the equivalent of almost $2,500 in 2020 dollars.

Prior to 1946, US currency had bills in circulation in $1, $5, $10, $20, $50, $100, $500, $1,000, $5,000 and $10,000 denominations. They stopped printing denominations above $100 in 1946 and withdrew them all from circulation by 1969 due to "lack of use."[3.1] That would explain why I'd never seen one. Well, partially.

Why is it that we no longer have large denomination bills in circulation? The U.S. Department of the Treasury web site and the Federal Reserve web site each give this reason:[3.1]

"On July 14, 1969, David M. Kennedy, the 60th Secretary of the Treasury, and officials at the Federal Reserve Board announced that they would immediately stop distributing currency in denominations of $500, $1,000, $5,000 and $10,000. Production of these denominations stopped during World War II. Their main purpose was for bank transfer payments. With the arrival of more secure transfer technologies, however, they were no longer needed for that purpose."

But there appears to be more to this story. The U.S. Embassy web site reveals that ". . . the last $500 - $1,000 bills were printed in 1945, and President Richard Nixon ordered them removed from circulation in 1969 in an effort to fight organized crime"[3.2]. Was this possibly the first shot fired in the modern war on cash? It's hard to be sure.

There are many internet references to the alleged "fact" that President Richard Nixon signed an Executive Order on July 14, 1969 removing all large bills from circulation.[3.3] A list of Presidential Executive Orders, however, does not show that any executive order was signed in July 1969, and none during Nixon's whole time in office, that involve changes to the currency.[3.4]

Nixon did address the Congress on that date regarding measures to be taken to control the sale and distribution of dangerous drugs in the U.S. In that address he stated that "The Department of the Treasury, through the Bureau of Customs, is charged with enforcing the nation's smuggling laws."[3.5]

On that same date in question, July 14, 1969, the U.S. Treasury and the Federal Reserve issued a joint press release announcing the withdrawal from circulation all currency in denominations greater than $100:[3.6]

> "The Treasury Department and the Federal Reserve System announced today that the issuance of currency in denominations of $500, $1,000, $5,000, and $10,000 will be discontinued immediately. Use of these large denominations has declined sharply over the last two decades and the need for them appears insufficient to warrant the added cost of production and custody of new supplies.
>
> "The large denomination notes were first authorized primarily for interbank transactions by an amendment to the Federal Reserve Act in 1918. With demand for them shrinking, printings of new notes of these denominations were discontinued in 1946, and the supply that was on hand at that time has now diminished to the point where continued issuance of such notes would require additional printings. Surveys have indicated that transactions for which the large denomination notes have been used could be met by other means, such as checks or $100 notes."

We now have three reasons from authoritative sources as to why the large bills were removed from circulation:

1. Large bills were no longer needed for between-bank transfers because of the development of electronic transfer systems.

2. The large bills were, for an unexplained reason, no longer demanded as often by the public.

3. The large bills were removed to fight organized crime by
    making it harder to carry large sums of money discreetly.

Which is the real reason? To say that the large bills were used
only for interbank settlements contradicts the claim that public
demand for those bills declined. If the large bills were intended
only for interbank settlement payments, why were they ever in
circulation? They must have been in circulation because they
were intended to be, which casts doubt on the government's official reason.

It seems conveniently coincidental that Nixon enlisted help of
the Treasury in 1969 to combat drug trafficking just as the Federal Reserve and the Treasury were announcing the withdrawal of
large denomination bills from circulation.

It would be fair to argue that the larger denominations should
be more in demand today than ever, considering the declining
value of the dollar. Inflation demands ever larger denominations
of currency.

Was this the first salvo in the modern war on cash? I'm not
sure, but it looks that way. The elimination of large bills was based
on the assertion that the main use for large bills was to facilitate
criminal transactions. This continues to be a main focus of the
war on cash.

CHAPTER 4

Academics Advocate for Eliminating Cash to Leverage Negative Interest Rates

---

❚❚ IT HAS LONG BEEN the dream of collectivists and technocratic elites to eliminate the semi-unregulated cash economy and black markets in order to maximise taxation and to fully control markets. If the cashless society is ushered in, they will have near complete control over the lives of individual people," wrote Patrick Henningsen of GlobalResearch.ca.

He goes on to say: "The cashless society is already here. The question now is how far will society allow it to penetrate and completely control each and every aspect of their day to day lives."

Henningsen also reports that contactless payment methods using smartphone technology are rapidly spreading and that "VISA now predicts that this new method will carry 50 percent of its transaction volume by the year 2020."[4.1]

It's bad enough that in the U.S., savers have been punished by the Federal Reserve's near-zero interest rate policy (ZIRP) in effect from December 2008 right through most of 2016 (and it is still abnormally low), and some of the elites are still salivating over the prospect of driving interest rates below zero (charging savers for keeping their money in the bank). The only way they can effectively get away with that is to eliminate cash.

In a cash-based economy, if the bank starts to charge depositors to keep their money in the bank, the depositors can withdraw their money in the form of cash and keep it elsewhere. In an economy without cash, the depositors have no choice but to suffer the negative interest rates (bank fees). This is actually quite similar to paying a fee for a checking account here in the U.S. Many people are choosing to "unbank" so they don't have to pay the fees. They are finding alternatives to banks. Imagine having the bank charge you to keep your money in a savings account. Rather than earning interest each month on your savings, you pay interest to the bank!

So who are these elites that want to deny you the use of cash? Well, one would be Mike Kimball, a professor of economics at the University of Michigan. In an article on Quartz (qz.com) entitled (and I'm not making this up) "How Paper Currency Is Holding the Recovery Back," he argues that if only banks could charge depositors to keep their cash in the vault, the economy would get better faster.[4.2]

The argument goes like this: if banks offer interest rates of two or three percent to depositors, the depositors will stockpile their money in the bank to take advantage of the interest they can earn. But to monetary tinkerers like Kimball, it would be better if people would invest the money to start businesses. He gives an example of a business that is thinking of building a factory in three years. It would be better, he writes, if they would build it now instead. So, he argues: "If someone would lend to them at an interest rate of -3.33% per year, the company could borrow $1 million to build the factory now, and pay back something like $900,000 on the loan three years later." After all, it would be much better to loan the factory money at -3.33% and lose a hundred grand over three years than it would be to keep your money in the bank and pay the bank -5% per year. In other words, in a negative interest scheme, you're actually paying the factory to borrow your money.

But why stop there? How about if everyone could borrow unlimited amounts of money and never have to pay it back? People would be starting businesses left and right. I would gladly do my part. I'd start by eating every meal at a restaurant. That would really boost the local economy. Then I'd buy a 4,000 square foot house for my extended family to live in. You know, my own "Kennedy Compound." Think of all the jobs that would create. We'd all be richer than Thurston Howell III. And we could all get off Gilligan's Island once and for all.

As long as cash exists, Kimball's plan won't work, since people will simply withdraw their cash from the bank rather than pay negative interest on it. Once they clean out all their cash from the bank, there will be a shortage of money for the bank to loan out, which will push interest rates up. That darn cash!

But I can hear some of you complaining: "Mike Kimball? A prof at some state university? What influence does he have on anything? Who cares what he thinks?" O.K., I hear you. So let me offer another "anti-cash" economist with a bit more influence: Willem Hendrik Buiter, PhD. Dr. Buiter is a Netherlands-born thinker with dual American-British citizenship. He's quite accomplished in economics and a Yale man to boot. From 2010 to 2018 he was the Global Chief Economist at Citigroup. Influencing interest rates is important to Citigroup in not a small way. If you have one of their credit cards, you already know that.

Buiter's resume and bio reveals an extensive list of associations with top European, British and American universities along with an impressive array of professorships, fellowships, and consultancies to various financial institutions, including the International Monetary Fund, the World Bank and Goldman Sachs. Buiter has published a great deal in the field of economics and has served in editorial positions of influential publications like the Journal of Financial Economic Policy and the Financial Times, and the journal International Economics and Economic Policy, just to name a few items listed on his lengthy curriculum vitae.

In case you still don't think he's influential enough to be of concern regarding your future use of cash, perhaps his association with various political bodies and think-tanks will persuade you. Remember, I got this information, not from some questionable "conspiracy theory" websites, but straight from his curriculum vitae posted on his website, www.willembuiter.com.[4.3] Here are a few of his associations: European Central Bank Shadow Council, Advisory Panel of the Economic and Monetary Committee of the Parliamentary Group of the Party of European Socialists, Member of the Brookings Panel on Economic Activity, Adviser to the House of Commons Select Service Committee of the Treasury and Civil Service, Co-chair of the Conference on Control and Economics, Princeton, New Jersey — the list goes on. Let's talk about his ideas and theories about cash and what he's promoting around the world to the banks and politicians that make decisions about your life.

On April 10, 2015, Bloomberg.com published an article entitled "Citi Economist Says It Might Be Time to Abolish Cash." Many financial and economic blogs picked up on this piece and parroted Buiter's policy proposals all over the internet. The Bloomberg article is based on a Citi Research paper authored by Buiter and published on April 9, 2015. Buiter's Citi Research paper is entitled: "High Time To Get Low: Getting Rid of the Lower Bound on Nominal Interest Rates."[4.4]

The "lower bound" is zero. As long as cash exists, it is nearly impossible to push interest rates much below zero: "The existence of the ELB [Effective Lower Bound, which means zero interest rate] is due to the existence of cash (bank notes) — a negotiable bearer instrument that pays a zero nominal interest rate. We view this constraint as undesirable and relatively easily avoidable from a technical, administrative and economic perspective."[4.5]

The problem as Buiter sees it is that the main tool central banks have to stimulate the economy is to cut interest rates to zero to encourage people to spend their money instead of putting it in a savings account. But what if banks have cut the rate to zero and people still refuse to spend? Then charge them to keep their money in the bank. Can you imagine buying a three-year CD for $10,000, and at the end of ten years you only get $8,500 back from the bank? That's what negative interest means. That's what Buiter and other economists, bankers, and bureaucrats are salivating over.

In the Citi Research paper, Buiter offers three ways to make it possible for interest rates to go below zero:

1. Abolish currency (cash).

2. Tax currency.

3. Remove the fixed exchange rate between cash and digital bank reserves. In other words, if your bank account has $1,000 and you go and close your account and demand your $1,000 in cash, the bank only gives you $950 or some similar amount that is less than your $1,000 balance.

None of these are new ideas, but they are enjoying a resurgence in popularity and application.

If cash is abolished and all of your money is electronic, there's no place you can keep it except in a bank. Your money is, in effect, held hostage by the bank and the government.

Buiter reports that out of the 69 central banks, four had negative interest rates as of April 2015 — the European Central Bank, the Swiss National Bank, the Swedish Riksbank, and the Danish Nationalbank — and many more have historically low interest rates.

Buiter emphasizes that limiting the interest rate to zero is undesirable and that adjusting interest rates below zero is preferable to quantitative easing (creating new money). In other words, he seems to be saying it's better to nudge depositors to spend the money in their bank accounts than it is to print new money and risk inflation and political blowback.

But Buiter knows that abolishing cash is not a popular idea, so he tries to get out in front of the problem by articulating the arguments against abolishing cash and labeling them "weak."

First, Buiter notes, people tend to resist change. But, he points out that at least in advanced economies there is an ever-growing range of electronic payment vehicles being used by the public. High-dollar "legitimate" transactions almost always occur electronically. So, he does not view this as a major stumbling block to the elimination of cash. This is where shaming comes into play. This is the notion that if you're using cash, you're somehow doing something illegitimate.

Second, he recognizes that poor people tend to use cash for most of their transactions. Buiter gets around this problem by suggesting that a limited quantity of small-denomination currency and coins be allowed to circulate for use by the poor — nothing larger than a five-dollar bill, he suggests. Alternatively, he suggests that the unbanked be "provided" with access to a bank account rather than allowing them to continue to use cash. By "provided" I can only assume he means "forced to use." We'll get more into this when I discuss the Better Than Cash Alliance and their efforts to move societies away from cash.

Third, central banks and governments would lose seigniorage revenue. What's that? Generally, it is the profit the government makes from the issuance of cash and other forms of money. Buiter isn't concerned about this; he seems to suggest that increased demand for other forms of money would be a substitute that would mitigate the loss of seigniorage revenue.

Fourth, loss of privacy and excessive intrusion by government. Buiter argues that the privacy lost will be outweighed by the reduction in crime. He makes the assumption that criminals are the biggest users of cash, even though he admits that "hard evidence is hard to come by." This is the same tired argument that because criminals use cash, the elimination of cash will reduce crime, or that if we make guns illegal we'll reduce the murder rate. How about we eliminate forks and spoons to eliminate obesity? Or we could eliminate cars and trucks and buses and trains and planes. Just think of all the lives we'd save. Honest people use cash too. Should we inconvenience everyone just to catch a few crooks? The best Buiter can promise is that giving up the anonymity of cash is "likely" to result in a positive net benefit to society. Likely.

Fifth, electronic payment systems create security risks. If humans can program it, other humans can hack into it. But Buiter has such faith in technology that he's confident we will stay one step ahead of the electronic crooks. Do you have that much faith? What's in your wallet?

Buiter concludes by saying that arguments against the elimination of cash are "weak." Nevertheless, he anticipates the "howls of horror" from ". . . German savers and their representatives." He blows off the concerns savers have of losing their savings to confiscatory negative interest rates by saying that they're not taking into account the difference between nominal and real interest rates and only focusing on the nominal (stated) rate of interest. The real interest rate is the nominal interest rate adjusted for inflation. So, for instance, if your bank is paying you 1% interest on your savings, but the rate of inflation is 4%, your money is actually losing 3% of its value each year. This would be akin to 3% negative interest. Buiter does not expand on his point, probably because it quickly gets complicated and theoretical. He does, however, acknowledge that lowering interest rates is "not always the right response to a situation of weak demand."

After four or five years of playing with negative interest rates, Buiter's theories have attracted some criticism. In 2019, Bloomberg reported that "Europe's unconventional experiment with negative interest rates to spur economic growth and inflation is looking like a trap."[4.6] After five years with negative interest rates, the European

Central Bank has fallen short of its goals. Negative interest rates are being ". . . blamed for weakening banks, expropriating savers, keeping dying companies on life support, and fueling an unsustainable surge in corporate debt and asset prices." In the US, negative interest rate theory has not taken hold yet, although it has received some support from the San Francisco Federal Reserve Bank in a published paper and from cited academics.

In December 2019, Sweden's central bank, the Riksbank, exited its negative interest rate policy by raising the repurchase rate back up to zero percent. Sweden was one of the first central banks to adopt negative interest rates and has now become the first to exit that strategy, effective January 2020. What was the reason for throwing off negative rates? One reason is Sweden's household debt ". . . which is among the highest in the world — with household debt exceeding 190% of disposable income — in part due to the low and negative interest rate environment that caused Swedes, as would be expected, to borrow with reckless abandon."[4.7]

Willem Buiter is not the only well-placed economist beating the drum to abolish cash. Kenneth Rogoff, a professor of economics and public policy at Harvard University, is of like mind. In an opinion piece in the *Financial Times*, Professor Rogoff showered his wisdom upon the masses in an article entitled "Paper Money Is Unfit for a World of High Crime and Low Inflation."[4.8] And once again we are hammered with the "cash = crime" theory. Rogoff's article is intended for a less scholarly audience. Unlike Buiter, to whom he refers in his article, Rogoff does not speak over the heads of the press by using monetary jargon.

Rogoff poses the question: "Has the time come to consider phasing out anonymous paper currency, starting with large-denomination notes?" Rogoff asserts that eliminating cash would "kill two birds with one stone," specifically, it would "eliminate the zero bound on . . . interest rates" while preventing people from "bailing out into cash." Further, it would "address the concern that a significant fraction, particularly of large-denomination notes, appears to be used to facilitate tax evasion and illegal activity."

Rogoff has not forgotten about all the Bitcoin proponents who think they're going to spoil the government's party. He writes: "Note that if governments do stop issuing anonymous currency, then they would probably have to ensure that the private sector did not proffer a Bitcoin-like substitute. Otherwise, illegal activities would proceed unabated, and the government would forfeit even the small inflation tax revenue it gets now."

Rogoff closes by proposing that "the right place to begin is by phasing out large denomination notes." I wonder what the reduction in tax evasion, money laundering and organized crime was after the elimination of the $500, $1,000, $5,000 and $10,000 Federal Reserve notes back in 1969? Somewhere around zero percent reduction, it would seem. There's no reason to believe there'd be any reduction in crime or tax evasion if cash were eliminated.

We've talked a lot about theory, but what are the chances that banks and governments will actually refuse to let depositors have their cash and force them to suffer negative interest rates? An article on the Schweizer Radio un Fernsehen (SRF) web site publicized a most uncomfortable situation that a Swiss pension fund manager found himself in with respect to the Swiss National Bank's negative interest rate policy.[4.9] To put this in context, understand that Switzerland is ranked number four on the list of countries with the most economic freedom in 2019 (the United States is considered less free with a ranking of #12, after falling from the #10 spot in 2014).[4.10]

As reported in SRF and reproduced in English on a variety of financial websites, a pension fund manager determined that the funds under his management were suffering negatively from the below-zero interest rate imposed by the Swiss National Bank, and that it was his fiduciary responsibility to pension fund investors to mitigate the losses. The fund manager determined that the fund would be better off if he orchestrated the withdrawal of the funds in cash and moved the money to a vault for safe-keep-ing. He issued a notice to the (as yet unnamed) bank letting them know of his intent to withdraw large amounts of cash. Here is the relevant part of the bank's response (according to SRF): "We are sorry, that within the time period specified, no solution corre-sponding to your expectations could be found."[4.11]

Hans Geiger, professor emeritus at the University of Zurich, a banking expert named in the article, opined that it was illegal for the bank to refuse such a request, since the pension fund ". . . has the contractual right to dispose of its money on demand." So how is the bank getting away with this?

The Swiss National Bank has recommended that ". . . in the col-lective interest of the Swiss economy," Swiss banks ". . . approach withdrawal demands in a restrictive manner." Perhaps there will be a legal challenge to what amounts to property seizure, but for the time being, pension fund investors have no choice but to watch their funds being whittled away by negative interest rates.

If this can happen in Switzerland, one of the most economically free countries in the world, it's not hard to imagine that it could (and will) happen in other countries, including the United States.

Lack of confidence in Greek banks has resulted in something approaching a run on the banks in 2015, with Greeks emptying out their accounts to the tune of $28 billion Euros. Greek frac-tional reserve banks quickly ended up in a cash crunch provoking the Greek government to slap a surcharge on all cash withdraw-als (but no financial reward for making deposits). The total cash held in Greek banks fell to a ten-year low.[4.12] The banking system has devolved into a scam where depositors are charged both for keeping their money in the bank and for taking it out. This is gov-ernment trying to drive north by flying south.

CHAPTER 5

Civil Societies Join the War on Cash

IT ISN'T ENOUGH THAT GOVERNMENTS, banks and academics collaborate in the war on cash, privacy, and individual liberty. Civil societies are now involved and paving the way for a cashless economy. These are large well-connected organizations that carefully coordinate their spending to exert influence around the world.

Klaus Schwab, in his "Future Role of Civil Society Report," defined civil society as "the area outside the family, market and state."[5.1] This, he writes, includes registered Non-Governmental Organizations (NGOs) and Civil Society Organizations (CSOs), online social media groups, social movements, religious organizations, labor unions and organizations, grassroots associations and local activities, and cooperatives controlled by their members. Schwab is the founder and Executive Chairman of the World Economic Forum, itself a non-governmental organization. More recently, Schwab has authored what is widely perceived to be the defining analysis of the Fourth Industrial Revolution — the alliance between Big Data, artificial intelligence, and technocracy, implemented through public-private partnerships. NGOs, like the United Nation Capital Development Fund, are leading the way in the war on cash.

Established in 1966, the United Nations Capital Development Fund (UNCDF), which defines itself as "The UN's capital investment agency for the world's 48 least developed countries," has thrown its influence into the fray by establishing a global program it calls the Better Than Cash Alliance.[5.2] Established in 2012, "The Better than Cash Alliance is an alliance of governments, private sector and development organizations committed to accelerating the shift from cash to electronic payments."[5.3] They aren't promoting a policy of choice between cash and digital payments: they state on their website's home page that they promote the transition from cash to digital payments by conducting research and developing tools to help in the transition while helping their members built digital payment economies.

Who are the members of the Better Than Cash Alliance? Here are a few of the "over 75" members who fund and participate in the mission, taken directly from betterthancash.org:

- Bill & Melinda Gates Foundation
- CARE
- Catholic Relief Services
- Citi Foundation
- Clinton Development Initiative
- Dominican Republic Government
- European Bank for Reconstruction and Development
- Gap, Inc.
- Federal Democratic Republic of Nepal
- Hashemite Kingdom of Jordan

- Inter-American Development Bank

- Islamic Republic of Pakistan

- Mastercard

- Many African and South American country governments

- The Coca-Cola Company

- United Nations Development Programme

- USAID

- Visa

Why are large global NGOs involved? Because eliminating cash isn't going to be easy. Liberty-minded people will resist. And while collective-minded folks are fairly easily convinced to restrain someone else's liberty, even the most hardcore collectivist will want to retain as much of his own liberty as possible. Governments and banks can put laws and policies in place in a bid to force compliance, but the gentle tide of social change washes over society through waves of foundation-funded propaganda and educational programming.

What is UNCDF and Better Than Cash Alliance's role in the gradual elimination of cash? According to the UNCDF web site, its role is: "Bringing about the shift to electronic payments on a global scale and ensuring that these benefits are maximized can be accelerated by an organization dedicated exclusively to providing global advocacy, knowledge sharing, collaboration and guidance on effective practices."

Spend some time on the website of the UNCDF web site or of any of its many partners, and you'll repeatedly encounter the term "financial inclusion." They want to include all people in the electronic financial system. This sounds like a laudable goal. After all, if they're not included, they're excluded. And being excluded doesn't sound fair. It's good for an individual to be able to choose between conducting a transaction in cash or electronically.

UNCDF defines "financial inclusion" this way:

"For UNCDF, Financial Inclusion is achieved when all individuals and businesses have access to and can effectively use a broad range of financial services that are provided responsibly, and at reasonable cost, by sustainable institutions in a well-regulated environment."[5.4]

To help achieve financial inclusion, UNCDF promotes its program, Better Than Cash Alliance, which is substantial enough to merit its own website and to attract significant "partner" participation and funding. The Better Than Cash Alliance produces plenty of reading material explaining what they're doing and why.

In its report, *The Journey Toward 'Cash Lite',* the Better Than Cash Alliance paraphrases this from another study: "The biggest opportunities for financial inclusion . . . come from financial service providers using the digital information generated by e-payments and receipts to form a profile of each individual customer. This digital profiling then enables providers to offer more appropriate and relevant products. Even beyond the use of e-payment records, businesses are starting to use other 'digital footprints,' such as mobile phone calling records and social network traffic, to offer credit to excluded groups."[5.5]

Let's unpack that last excerpt from the report. It says the "biggest opportunities" for financial inclusion come from digital profiling: tracking the buying behaviors of individual consumers to better target them with marketing, and invading their privacy by following their digital footprints. Included in a consumer's digital footprint are mobile phone calling records as well as their social media activity. One of the stated goals is "to offer credit to excluded groups." Examining a consumer's mobile phone records is one method for determining credit risk, and even for discovering the user's gender.[5.6]

Note the creation of two groups of consumers by the use of language: those consumers who are "included" by having their electronic transactions tracked and used for marketing and the making of consumer loans, and those who are "excluded" by engaging in private transactions with cash and not by going into debt.

There is nothing wrong with giving "excluded" consumers the opportunity to engage in electronic transactions. The concern is that the choice to use cash is gradually being excluded, to borrow their terminology. *The Journey Toward Cash-Lite's* concluding paragraph says it all:

". . . financially included individuals exercise real choices over how they pay . . . The choices they make cause the usage of cash, with all its often poorly understood and usually misallocated costs and benefits, to dwindle. With that end goal in mind, governments, businesses and donors can focus their energy and resources in purposeful, coordinated actions which can shift the payment landscape, even in the most cash heavy societies today."

They freely admit that the end goal is to "cause the usage of cash . . . to dwindle."

It's interesting to note that costs associated with the use of cash (printing money, for instance, or keeping it safe) are poorly understood and misallocated, whereas the costs of electronic money (fees for transactions, service charges, interest on loans) are viewed as lower, better understood, properly allocated and, therefore, desirable.

One of the largest NGOs dedicated to financial inclusion is the Mastercard Foundation. This is a Canadian private foundation which also operates as a 501(c)(4) social welfare organization under US law. It is also has foreign registration in Rwanda and Ghana. The Mastercard Foundation was funded in 2006 when Mastercard gifted approximately 16% of its shares to its own foundation.[5.7] Those 112,181,762 restricted shares are now about 10% of total stock holdings and were worth over 17 billion dollars on December 31, 2018 according to the company's audited financials. The foundation claims to operate independently with respect to Mastercard.[5.8]

The primary geographical focus of activities and spending of the Mastercard Foundation is Africa, and the focus is on "financial inclusion" of poor populations. Their website explains their goals for Africa — to enable 30 million young people in Africa, especially young women, to get jobs and get out of poverty. They will do this by:

- Improving the quality of education and vocational training so young people will have the skills employers need;

- Leverage technology to connect employers and job seekers and drive growth; and

- Enable entrepreneurs and small businesses to expand through access to financial services.

Certainly these sound like laudable and charitable goals. But it's the third item on the list — access to financial services — that seems a little self-serving.

Each year, the Mastercard Foundation holds a Symposium on Financial Inclusion. A video from the 2017 symposium featured a panel segment called "Financial Inclusion in a Dynamic West African Context." Edward Effah, Group CEO of Fidelity Bank Ghana Ltd. and panel participant, reported that since 2010, Ghana has reduced the percentage of their population with no access to financial services from 50% to 24%. The major game-changer has been the introduction of "mobile money," by which he refers to using smart phones to conduct digital payment transactions. Ghana, in 2017, had 10 million "mobile money" subscribers. He goes on to list all the services being introduced to Ghana to promote financial inclusion, including mobile money, lending products, national I.D. cards, a digital addressing system (to pinpoint where digital subscribers live), credit, insurance, and micro-finance.[5.9] The Mastercard Foundation is introducing the debt-based economic system to the third world, thereby growing the market share and customer base of Mastercard. The fact that the Foundation may be improving lives and providing opportunity is great, but its role in increasing dependence on digital payments directly benefits Mastercard and its shareholders. Mr. Effah notes that despite the fact that both banks and phone providers are operating in the digital money market, it is not a zero-sum game. Market size is increasing, and there are plenty of profits to go around. Money that was previously held outside of banks is now becoming digital and is held by the banks. Whatever Mastercard is doing, it is obviously working. Mastercard stock share prices have increased from around $90 in 2015 to around $300 in 2020. Dividend payouts have correspondingly increased.

Although the anti-cash, pro-digital alliances use the term "inclusion" to mean expanding access to digital payment systems while reducing cash usage, the G4S.com Global Cash Report for 2018 defines the idea of "inclusion" differently when it states: "All over the world people prefer to use cash, and for many people it is the only viable payment method. Businesses that stop using cash are excluding a material portion of the society and risk losing customers."[5.10]

An entire book could be written on the role nonprofits and governments are playing in the gradual exclusion of cash as a choice, but I've provided evidence that these entities are key strategists and combatants in the war on cash. And it isn't just one or two non-governmental groups involved. "The Consultative Group to Assist the Poor is a global partnership of "more than 30 leading development organizations" that seek to advance financial inclusion and is housed at the World Bank."[5.11] They include: Mastercard Foundation, African Development Bank, Bill & Melinda Gates Foundation, Credit Suisse, European Investment Bank, Global Affairs Canada, MetLife Foundation, The World Bank, USAID, and the United Nations Capital Development Fund, among others.

The machinery operating to eliminate cash is a multi-billion dollar juggernaut.

CHAPTER 6

Use Cash? You Must Be a Criminal

DAVE BIRCH, AN ELECTRONIC payments system developer in the UK, gave a TED talk in favor of eliminating cash entirely.[6.1] One of his arguments was that it facilitates the implementation of monetary policy, particularly negative interest rates. Negative interest is something we have not yet experienced in the U.S., but some European banks are not only refusing to pay interest to their depositors, but also charging their depositors a fee to keep cash savings in the bank. This is called negative interest.

If Dave Birch is an indication of what we're up against, we have a dark future indeed. In his 2015 TEDx talk he put forth, correctly I believe, that it would be the mobile phone that gets rid of cash. This pleases him, as his position is that no transactions should be in cash, going so far as to say that anyone who pays in cash should go to jail because they are facilitating tax fraud. I'm not making this up. He put forth an idea that involves using smart phones. One could make a payment via a smart phone app in "light coins" where one's identity and all aspects of the transaction would be public. Any company could "data mine" the transaction, which would make the transaction free to the parties involved, since the data would be sold. Another choice would be to pay in "dark coins." This could be used to pay for illegal drugs or prostitution. All aspects of the transaction would be private, but there would be a 20 percent withholding tax that would be automatically sent to the government. This way, he says, the government would cash in on the black market, which is not currently paying taxes. It appears to be, in effect, a sales tax on private transactions. In that case the government would then become dependent on the black market for revenue. How's that for a conflict of interest?

Our government and our media have done a great job of associating cash with crime, right down to pitting neighbor against neighbor. I live in a city that prides itself on having a great variety of restaurants advertising "The Best Cuban Sandwich in Town." Recently I discovered one near my house that had outstanding reviews online except for one minor quibble that a few people had: the restaurant does not accept debit or credit cards or any other form of electronic payment. It's cash only. This review from one experienced restaurant reviewer jumped out at me: "There is nothing more annoying than going to an establishment and them telling you that they only take cash . . . stop scaming [sic] the government and pay your taxes like every other business does . . ." Apparently, it didn't occur to the reviewer that there might be legitimate reasons for not accepting cards. Card processors take a roughly 3% bite out of every transaction plus an additional 30 cents or so. That adds up quickly if you have a large number of transactions of less than ten dollars as a small sandwich shop might have. Credit card fraud is another reason to shy away from plastic. Or perhaps the owner just doesn't like supporting the big credit lenders who charge exorbitant interest and fees to consumers and who are rapidly sucking people into debt slavery.

Let's have a look at some of the common reasons given to eliminate cash from the economy that don't involve monetary policy:

- Eliminating cash would make it difficult to conduct black market transactions and would increase tax revenues by forcing criminals to pay tax.

- Eliminating cash would reduce crimes like armed robbery (especially bank robberies).

- Eliminating cash would make it harder for people to avoid paying taxes.

- Eliminating cash would make it easy for the government to monitor what people purchase.

- Eliminating cash would reduce terrorism.

Now let's consider why keeping some cash around might be a good idea and why some of the reasons to eliminate cash are not as desirable as they may appear:

Eliminating cash will cause the black market to conduct business either in some other country's currency, or by using some other "commodity," like silver, gold, ammunition, pharmaceuticals, tobacco products, women, children, etc. This would most likely increase the market for stolen goods to be used as barter. As I mentioned, in some inner-city neighborhoods, stolen Tide laundry detergent has become a popular item to barter for drugs.[6.2]

Honeybuns are used as currency in Florida prisons. Those sticky sweet pastries are used as a medium of exchange. Florida prison inmates purchase 270,000 honeybuns per month in 2010. George Alec Robinson paid his public defenders in honeybuns after they saved him from the electric chair. Football bets are paid in honey buns. A Naples, Florida, bail bondsman paid compensation in honeybuns to inmates for referral business. Stealing a honeybun can get you killed.[6.3] Note that due to their short life span, honeybuns are not a good store of wealth. Nevertheless, they serve the purpose of facilitating exchange transactions.

The belief that armed robberies will be reduced seems at best to be fanciful. It is true that armed robberies of banks would decline if no cash were available, and ATM robberies would likely decline. But criminals would still target people for robberies and take their smart-phones, credit cards, jewelry, and whatever else of value people carry. Even if you don't carry cash, thieves are experts at converting your stuff into cash, drugs or some other item of value.

Certainly, without cash, credit card fraud will continue to increase ad infinitum. I almost always pay for restaurant meals and gasoline with cash, and increasingly I pay cash for groceries. There are a number of stores I'll never use a debit card in again after their systems were hacked. Don't most people have a twinge of insecurity when buying online from an unknown retailer? I do. But I don't get that feeling when spending cash. It's liberating to buy something with cash, knowing your purchase is private as long as you don't offer your phone number when asked by the cashier. In the future, privacy will be difficult even when using cash as facial recognition software is adopted by merchants.

Privacy expert J.J. Luna offers several advantages to making routine purchases with cash instead of with credit or debit cards or checks.[6.4]

- Impulse purchases are virtually eliminated. If you don't have the money on hand, you can't buy it.

- You don't have to make monthly payments on debt, and you don't incur interest expense and bank overdraft fees.

- Cash purchases often qualify for discounts.

- Using cash is one of the best protections against identity theft. And you won't have to produce a driver's license or reveal your home address.

- If the electronic payments system goes down (like after a hurricane), having cash on hand will allow you to continue to buy food and meet your basic needs. Despite what some people say, most stores have systems in place to accept cash payments when their electronic payment terminals are down. Cash is still king.

Note that none of the above reasons would indicate criminal intent.

Some point out that cash is not a good store of wealth and that banks and the government should not encourage people to keep savings in cash. Charging people a monthly fee to deposit their cash savings is a good way to discourage the keeping of cash. The argument is that society should want people to invest their savings in businesses, not to hoard cash. This argument might work in some countries, but in the United States of America we're a society based on the primacy of the individual, not of society. It isn't what my neighbors think about what I should do with my money that matters. What matters is what I want to do with my money without manipulation by governments and bankers. And if cash is not a good store of wealth, then keeping money in the bank at negative interest isn't either. Is there something wrong with storing wealth? Suppose I'd like to save money for a down payment on a house. It might take a decade to do that. People need a way to store their wealth. What about saving for retirement? Punishing savers is a bad idea. If cash isn't a good store of wealth, perhaps we should ask why it isn't, and what could be done to fix that.

What about tax dodges? When people are able to do business in cash, anonymously, it's easier for them to evade taxes. This is true. But there are problems with this concern. With the economy in shambles and rampant inflation, high taxes, and pervasive unemployment and underemployment, the only way many people avoid homelessness is to work for cash "under the table."

If those people and businesses were forced into the tax system by the elimination of cash, homelessness and despair would increase dramatically, increasing the burden on the government to provide homeless shelters, food stamps, medical care and counseling services. Nowhere is this more in evidence than in countries like Argentina, where the underground economy thrives in the face of high taxation and economic despair and American dollars are in high demand. With the elimination of cash, small businesses that can't afford to join the tax collection system would stop hiring day labor and independent contractors, and many of these under-the-table jobs would disappear, driving people even further into despair and dependence on government handouts. I venture to predict that the suicide rate among men would increase as well.

CHAPTER 7

Give Up Cash, Give Up Privacy, Give Up Control

LET'S GET TO THE main reasons that eliminating cash would be a disaster for society — especially American society. These reasons create the only argument necessary to refute the notion that a cashless economy is a good idea. A cashless economy relies entirely on electronic transactions. These transactions are transmitted via the internet, cell phone networks, and satellites. All such transactions have electronic documentation that identifies every aspect of the transaction, including who made the purchase, what was purchased, when, where purchased, and from whom it was purchased. The transaction is "data mined." This means that if Mary buys a firearm and ammunition, then makes a donation to the Republican Party and to Judicial Watch, the government has access to that information. If John pays a visit to a local adult entertainment establishment, there is a permanent, discoverable electronic record. If Rodrigo suddenly starts buying a lot of potting soil and grow lights and irrigation hose, the government can be informed. Rodrigo is simply into growing his own vegetables year-round, but to the government he's automatically suspected of growing marijuana. He will be surveilled and probably be the recipient of a "no-knock" search warrant at three in the morning by a S.W.A.T. team in full battle regalia.[7.1] These people then become easy targets for politicians and special interest activists. Do you think that is farfetched? It's already happening.

With all transactions taking place electronically, you will lose all privacy. Your health insurance company will know how much beer you drink, how many candy bars and donuts you buy, and which over-the-counter medications you take (which might indicate health risks that will increase your premiums). Certainly there are benefits to having a completely transparent life. It's like not being able to tell a lie. Just as with targeted internet ads that seem to follow you from one site to another, businesses will be able to target you for your complete and unfiltered buying behavior and history. They will know more about you than does your spouse or your parents. Most people, I hope, would conclude that the price of the loss of privacy is too high.

Giving up cash doesn't just mean you're giving up your privacy. It means you're completely giving up control over your money to banks and to the government. With the click of a mouse your bank and brokerage accounts can be closed and emptied. In a world without cash, the only way to conduct business legally is to have a bank account. If the government decides they don't like your business (maybe you're selling political campaign T-shirts for the "wrong" side), they can close your accounts. Or perhaps you sell fireworks, or coins, or ammunition, or you operate a pawn shop. But those are legal businesses. Those people aren't doing anything wrong, so they don't have anything to worry about, right?

Ever heard of Operation Choke Point? Most people haven't. But it's shutting down businesses and ruining people's lives.[7.2]

Operation Choke Point is the result of an Obama executive order authorizing the Department of Justice to put pressure on banks and third-party lenders to refuse to lend to or maintain accounts for legal businesses and industries that the government does not approve of as well as some which may be engaged in illegal activities. The intent seemed worthy — to prevent fraudulent business practices, particularly against "payday lenders." But like so many government power-backed initiatives, it quickly became an abusive scheme that preyed upon the innocent. Through Operation Choke Point, the Federal Deposit Insurance Corporation (FDIC) equates legal and regulated activities like coin dealers and firearms and ammunition sales with illegal activities like Ponzi schemes, debt consolidation scams, and the sale of drug paraphernalia.[7.3]

In 2011, the FDIC released a report entitled "Managing Risks in Third-Party Payors" that revealed 30 of the high-risk merchant categories being targeted by the Department of Justice. Here's the list:[7.4]

- Ammunition sales
- Cable box de-scramblers
- Coin dealers
- Credit card schemes
- Credit repair services
- Dating services
- Debt consolidation scams
- Drug paraphernalia
- Escort services
- Firearms sales
- Fireworks sales
- Get rich products
- Government grants

- Home-based charities
- Lifetime guarantees
- Lifetime memberships
- Lottery sales
- Mailing lists/ personal information
- Money transfer networks
- Online gambling
- Payday loans
- Pharmaceutical sales
- Ponzi schemes
- Pornography
- Pyramid-type sales
- Racist materials
- Surveillance equipment
- Telemarketing
- Tobacco sales
- Travel clubs

The FDIC has rescinded the list, but the U.S. Consumer Coalition has stated that ". . . The real threat from Operation Choke Point never came from the official guidance delivered through financial institutions letters issued by the FDIC. Operation Choke Point uses the bank examination process to intimidate banks into ending relationships with so-called 'high risk' merchants. The guidance in the FIL [FDIC's Financial Institution Letter] means nothing if examiners do not stop their intimidation of banks during the examination process, a fact that was proven in the audio tapes of Heritage Credit Union we obtained and released last month."[7.5]

A Congressional Oversight Committee concluded in a December 2014 report that ". . . there was no articulated justification or rationale for the original list of "high-risk merchants." Further, it concluded that Operation Choke Point is an abuse of the Department's statutory authority, and that as a result of Operation Choke Point, banks are indiscriminately terminating relationships with legal and legitimate merchants across a variety of business lines.[7.6]

In the face of criticism and actions by legislators, the FDIC issued guidance to its employees regarding the denial of banking services to businesses based on the industry they represent. As reported by the Competitive Enterprise Institute, "One of the ways Choke Point has proceeded has been via supervisors issuing veiled threats or direct but unwritten comments that suggest a banking institution should stop doing business with a client. As a result, there has been no paper trail within the [Obama] administration directly linking the closure of bank accounts with Operation Choke Point."[7.7]

If you own or work for one of the above industries, you may well find yourself cut off from banking services, causing your business to fail or causing you to lose your job and your home. During research for this book, I found the following (unedited) comment on a story about Operation Choke Point on the American Banker website:

"Dear God! I would have thought if I opened a site like Operation Choke Point that it was just a stupid site that believes in all the conspiracy theories. However I deliberately looked this up after my daughter's banker told her that is why her account was closed. She works for a topless club in Hollywood, CA. Her bank is Chase. This is the most frightening thing that has ever happened. I am now a believer in what havoc Obama has reaped on American people. When are people going to realize that this is not a joke or the result of hysterical people. This is for real."[7.8]

The government pressured Chase Bank to close a woman's personal bank account because she worked for a topless club, which is a legal business activity.

In Hyannis, Massachusetts, Mark Cohen, owner of Powder-horn Outfitters, a gun retailer, was denied a line of credit by TD Bank. The bank manager told him that ". . . the bank is turning you down because you sell guns." Never mind that he had a longtime relationship with the bank and had known the bank manager for over 20 years, according to an article in the Daily Caller, after being dropped by TD Bank, Cohen did some research and realized the bank was pressured by Operation Choke Point. Quoting Cohen: "It's frightening the way the government can come in and say you don't have a right to exist and shut off your funding." Cohen fought back by closing his business accounts with TD and by informing his customers, hundreds of whom also closed their TD accounts.[7.9]

The Department of Justice is also targeting the adult entertainment industry by closing the personal bank accounts of actors in that industry as well as the accounts of their spouses.[7.10] This despite the fact that on the whole, these adult businesses are operating within the law.

Peggy Craig, owner of Michael's Pawn and Gun in Fruitland, Florida called TD bank to open a line of credit to finance inventory and finance an advertising campaign. The bank representative pulled up the Facebook page of Michael's Pawn and Gun and learned that the store sells . . . guns. Ms. Craig was denied the chance to apply for credit. The bank told her "We can't lend to anyone who sells firearms."[7.11]

In Brooksville, Florida, American Gun & Pawn had its accounts closed by Sun Trust Bank. Owner Steve Champion believes Sun Trust cut him off because of Operation Chokepoint. Sun Trust, as one might expect, told Champion that the closures had nothing to do with Operation Chokepoint, but were "due to increased regulation" as related by Champion in various statements made to WFLA, a local NBC affiliate.[7.12]

On August 8, 2014, SunTrust issued a news release that stated: "We have decided to discontinue banking relationships with three types of businesses — specifically payday lenders, pawn shops and dedicated check-cashers — due to compliance requirements."[7.13] While SunTrust maintains that it is targeting pawn shops, not gun dealers, Champion said that a bank representative referred to the letter he received as a "gun letter" and said they were sent to gun shops all over the nation. Does it not seem too coincidental that Operation Chokepoint is known to specifically target those same three industries, is known to put pressure on banks to stop maintaining accounts with those businesses, and SunTrust, being a bank, is closing accounts of these businesses; yet we are directed to believe there is no connection. While WFLA reports that neither regulators nor banks want to answer questions, several members of Congress have weighed in and agree that American Gun & Pawn's closure is part of Operation Chokepoint.[7.14]

Ultimately, it makes no difference whether it is gun dealers or pawn shops that are being targeted, or both. Both of these industries are legal businesses and are entitled to conduct business within the law. And banks, being private businesses, certainly have a lawful right to decline to do business with industries that they think are too high risk (as long as they don't discriminate based on age, race, gender, or sexual orientation of course). It is not the place of the government to pick and choose which lawfully operated businesses are allowed to have bank accounts. As has been observed, denying these businesses access to the financial services system forces them to do business only in cash — which is what the government is trying to discourage.

Writer and documentary film producer G. Edward Griffin, in his book *The Creature from Jekyll Island*, predicts the following future scenario: "Electronic transfers gradually replace cash and checking accounts. This permits UN agencies to monitor the financial activities of every person. A machine-readable ID card is used for that purpose. If an individual is red-flagged by any government agency, the card does not clear, and he is cut off from all economic transactions and travel. It is the ultimate control."[7.15] It's easy to see how Operation Chokepoint and any derivative policies that may follow are not far off from Griffin's scenario.

As public comments on news articles regularly note, the problem is not the banks, but rather the heavy-handedness of the government in its attempt to use banks to achieve its objective, which is to go after businesses that do a lot of business with cash customers. How long will it be until you cannot legally buy a gun with cash?

As I was researching this story on the WFLA website, the search results just for "American Gun & Pawn," yielded this year-old unrelated story: "SunTrust has agreed to pay nearly $1 billion to resolve allegations that it underwrote and endorsed faulty mortgage loans, the Justice Department announced Tuesday." SunTrust ". . . underwrote bad loans between 2006 and 2012, gave borrowers false and misleading information about the status of foreclosure proceedings and charged unauthorized fees." That story, like several others related to SunTrust, has disappeared from the WFLA website.[7.16]

Could it be that this large settlement with Eric Holder's Justice Department in July 2014 precipitated the SunTrust news release in August 2014 announcing that it would discontinue banking relationships with payday lenders, pawn shops, and check cashing businesses? Is this settlement an example of how SunTrust was pressured to comply with Operation Chokepoint? I'm not saying they are related; I'm just asking the question. Perhaps banks are the high-risk businesses, not the pawn and gun stores.

But not to worry: more than 30 members of Congress sent letters to the Federal Deposit Insurance Corporation (FDIC) and to the Department of Justice (DOJ) requesting an investigation into Operation Chokepoint, which is ". . . an operation in which the FDIC and DOJ intimidate financial institutions from offering financial services to certain licensed, legally-operating industries the government doesn't like in an attempt to choke off those industries from our country's banking system." A thorough investigation into the behavior of the FDIC and the DOJ will be conducted by — the FDIC and the DOJ.[7.17]

Frank Keating, president and CEO of the American Bankers Association, as well as being a former FBI agent, U.S. attorney, and associate attorney general of the United States, wrote an op-ed in the Wall Street Journal in which he asks: ". . . why is the Justice Department telling bankers to behave like policemen and judges?" He explains that "Operation Chokepoint is asking banks to identify customers who may be breaking the law or simply doing something government officials don't like. Banks must then 'choke off' those customers' access to financial services, shutting down their accounts."[7.18] Whatever happened to due process of law?

Representatives Blaine Luetkemeyer of Missouri and Sean Duffy of Wisconsin have been some of the most active legislators trying to expose and shut down Operation Chokepoint. So far, however, efforts to pass legislation to end Operation Choke Point have failed. In December 2017, the House of Representatives passed (395-2) the Financial Institution Customer Protection Act (H.R. 2706), which was introduced by Luetkemeyer. This bill, if it became law, would end Operation Choke Point. Unfortunately, the bill was not passed by the Senate. It was reintroduced in the House as H.R. 189 in January 2019 and has a 3% chance of being enacted according to Skopos Labs.[7.19]

Should the government be able to shut off your access to money just because they don't like your business? If a business is breaking the law, there's a process for gathering evidence, charging them, convicting them and punishing them. The Justice Department should use that process.

This is the problem with allowing the government access to all of your private transactions. If the currently serving administration decides you're involved, however tangentially, in an industry it does not favor, it can put you out of business without due process of law, even though your business activities are lawful. If all transactions are electronic, they can be monitored or stopped. If there is no cash, you have no money if the government, banks, or payment processors cut off your access to the electronic payment systems.

A disturbing trend in recent years involves banks and other private businesses, usually under pressure from activist groups, cutting certain individuals off from access to banking and credit in an attempt to silence them, and cutting off their access to services.

Examples:

Martina Markota, a video host for conservative news website Rebel Media, had its Chase Bank account closed.

Joe Biggs, an independent reporter, Army combat veteran, and Purple Heart recipient also had his bank account closed by Chase Bank.

Enrique Tarrio, chairman of the Proud Boys activist group and owner of a website selling "provocative political merchandise," had his bank account closed by Chase Bank.[7.20]

Lara Loomer, a conservative investigative journalist, was banned by PayPal, Twitter, Medium, Uber, Lyft, Uber Eats, GoFundMe, Venmo, and MGM Resorts for being outspoken on the wrong issues and asking the wrong questions.[7.21] For Loomer and others I've mentioned in this chapter, even partially losing access to electronic payment systems has been devastating. It's not a theory for them. It's real life. Loomer writes: "How am I supposed to pay my bills? Am I supposed to be homeless? They want me to die from all of the pressure and stress of not being able to live freely in America." Fortunately, Loomer and the others still have access to cash. What if they didn't?

Robert Spencer of jihadwatch.org was banned from the Patreon platform in 2018 because of a demand from Mastercard, which apparently processes payments for Patreon.[7.22]

The biggest payment processor, **PayPal**, is on record saying that it will deny access to the PayPal payment processing system to anyone who may fall afoul of its social justice platform, with little chance for appeal.[7.23] Other financial processing platforms like GoFundMe and YouCaring have also banned right-leaning groups and individuals from using their services.[7.24]

PayPal has also cancelled the accounts of Infowars, British activist Tommy Robinson, several heavy metal music labels, James Goddard (leader of the British Yellow Vests), and social networks Gab and BitChute, which are alternatives to Twitter and YouTube, respectively.

For many decades, banks and other financial institutions have not discriminated against people or groups because of their political beliefs. Even convicted felons have had bank accounts, mortgages and credit cards (to the extent they were otherwise in good standing). Cutting people off from the banking and electronic payments system is an alarming new development that has the potential to destroy any person and any company when there is no option to use cash.

Running a business with nationwide or worldwide customers is impossible without electronic transactions. Running a business locally without having access to banks and payment processors is very difficult, but it can be done as a last resort. Without cash, there is no last resort.

The privacy and personal empowerment inherent in the ability to use cash cannot be duplicated with electronic transactions. Some would argue that crypto currencies like Bitcoin offer privacy. This is a foolhardy belief. One need look no further than to the Twitter feed of @NeonaziWallets created by John Bambenek, a cybersecurity expert and lecturer at the University of Illinois. He has created a "an automated feed of bitcoin transactions involving suspected neonazi [sic] or altright [sic] extremist wallets." If you think cryptocurrency is private, I urge you to view the Neonazi BTC Tracker here: https://twitter.com/NeonaziWallets

Others, like the payment process developer in the U.K. I wrote about earlier, can argue that certain electronic transactions could remain private, while providing for an automatic withholding of 20% which is transmitted to the IRS. The problem with this scheme in the United States of America is that it would more or less have to assume that all private transactions are fully taxable, which they are not. Further, whose tax ID number would get credit for the withholding? It would have to function as a non-refundable sales tax. A 20% sales tax. Schemes like this quickly get complicated, and the level of inconvenience visited upon the public and the ramifications of unintended consequences create a rip in the economic and social fabric that is likely to do more harm than good. These electronic payment schemes also depend on trust in the people running the system. Do you have that trust?

CHAPTER 8

Risks of Cash: Theft by Inflation

FOR PEOPLE WHO HAVE wealth or property, however small the amount, there is always a risk of loss. Cash is particularly susceptible to theft, loss, destruction, confiscation by governments, devaluation by inflation, and it creates an attractive target for lawsuits.

We can guard against theft and loss by keeping cash in a home safe or in the bank's safe. We can shield cash from lawsuits by purchasing insurance. But can we protect our cash from confiscation by governments either physically through taxation, outright seizure or through inflation?

Inflation is one of those things that the average person does not understand. Simply put, inflation means that dollars are worth less now than they were before. A dollar buys less today than it did yesterday. This means that prices increase to accommodate the lower worth of the dollar.

But how can the dollar be worth less one day than the next. Isn't that just trickery? Isn't that just arbitrary? No, not really.

Inflation is a real event that happens when the amount of goods that people want to buy decreases relative to the amount of dollars that are available to spend. I know, that sounds like something from your boring economics class at the community college, but bear with me.

Imagine that a hurricane sweeps through the Gulf of Mexico and shuts down all the oil wells for a month. What happens to the supply of oil? The amount of oil available to make gasoline decreases dramatically, leading to a sharp decrease in the amount of gasoline available at your local gas station. But people still want the gasoline. And they still have the same amount of money to pay for it because the hurricane did not destroy dollars. So, just like on eBay, people bid up the price of gasoline. There's lots of money (relatively speaking), but a lot less gasoline to buy even though people still need the same amount (or more) as before the hurricane. This is a type of inflation. The amount of money available to buy gasoline in the affected area exceeds the amount of gasoline available to purchase. A dollar buys less gasoline after the hurricane than it did before.

The same result could occur if, instead of the supply of gasoline going down, the supply of dollars went up. People would have more money to spend and might start taking more vacations and doing a lot more driving. They would demand more gasoline and once again the price of gasoline would go up. How would the supply of dollars go up, you ask? The government creates new money all the time as part of its monetary policy. You've heard of Quantitative Easing? It's the latest term for the government and Federal Reserve "printing" more money and injecting it into the economy in the vain hopes of "kick-starting" the economy.

When the government prints too much money, it increases the amount of dollars in the economy without increasing the amount of stuff people want to buy. This makes all the dollars worth less relative to the goods. This is inflation. And it robs you just as if someone put a gun to your head and made you hand over part of your checking account. It's a hidden tax. But the inflation tax is not progressive, meaning it does not hit the rich harder. Inflation is the cruelest tax because it takes desperately needed purchasing power away from the poor and from retirees who are living on savings and a fixed income. Just as when you add water to fresh orange juice, it dilutes the taste of the juice, when the government adds too many dollars to the economy, it dilutes the purchasing power of all the dollars.

The hurricane is a limited example of short-lived inflation. Eventually the oil wells come back online and the supply of gasoline increases to normal levels and prices come back down. But what happens when there is a nationwide increase in dollars relative to the goods people want to buy? When the government creates lots of new dollars, it dilutes the purchasing power of all dollars. This means prices go up. Your money (including your cash) is worth less than before the new money was created. That's inflation.

CHAPTER 9

Consumers, Prices, and Cash

LET'S HAVE A CLOSER look at how inflation affects you and your cash. Government economists attempt to measure and track inflation. The government has created something called a "market basket" of about 80,000 goods and services, and it tracks price changes for those items. The changes in prices in this market basket of goods allows the government to create a measure of inflation that it calls the Consumer Price Index (CPI). It's also known as the "cost of living index."

If you search for "Inflation Calculator," you'll find entertaining web pages that will show you exactly how inflation has been squeezing you over the course of your life.

For the official Bureau of Labor Statistics inflation calculator,[9.1] go to http://www.bls.gov/data/inflation_calculator.htm

For this demonstration, that's the one I'll use. Bear in mind that some economists dispute the validity of the government's

CPI calculation, charging that it understates actual inflation;[9.2] others say it doesn't measure inflation at all, but only changes in buying behavior.[9.3]

Here's how the calculator works: you enter a dollar amount, a date in the past, and a date in the future. It then calculates the change in purchasing power over that period.

When I graduated high school in 1978, the federal minimum wage was $2.65 per hour. When I plug those numbers into the calculator and choose 2020 as a future date, the calculator tells me that in order to have the same level of purchasing power today that the $2.65 had in 1978, I would need to earn $10.94 per hour. The actual federal minimum wage as of January 2020 is $7.25. So the federal minimum wage has not quite kept up with inflation. Various states have their own minimum wage, which often exceeds the federal minimum.

The cost of ground beef in 1963 was about 45 cents per pound. Adjusted for inflation, ground beef should cost about $3.82 per pound today. While prices vary considerably based on market conditions, I typically pay about $4.99 per pound at my supermarket. That's largely the effects of inflation. I could probably get it considerably cheaper at a wholesale club, but they didn't have those in 1963.

The government has been robbing us with inflation for decades by creating too much money. Of course, as long as your salary keeps up with inflation, it's not a problem, right? Well, not exactly. Inflation punishes savers.

If you put $10,000 into a safe in 1990, and you took it out to spend it in 2020, it will have lost $4,939 of its purchasing power — stolen by inflation.

Or, if you put $10,000 in a savings account in 2001, you would have earned so little interest that the value of your money in 2020 would have diminished almost the same as if you put it in a safe where it earned zero interest. Some people might get lucky by putting their money in the right stocks or mutual funds and get a return that beats inflation, but most won't be (unless they're members of Congress),[9,4] especially if the market happens to be down when they need to withdraw the money. Or if someone like John Corzine or Bernie Madoff decides to just take their money; that could be a problem.

It is often observed that the US Dollar has lost about 96% of its purchasing power since 1913. Some critics of this observation say that it does not matter, since in the real world, people earn interest, dividends, or capital gains on their savings and investments. Average investment earnings over the last century have been more than enough to offset the effects of inflation. This may be true for many savers and investors. But it ignores what would have happened with zero inflation.

One dollar in 1913 had the same purchasing power as $26.32 in 2020. That means if you put your dollar in the bank in 1913, you'd have to earn 3.10% interest every year just to keep up with inflation — just to have the same purchasing power in 2020 that you had in 1913. In other words, you didn't gain anything, you have the same purchasing power you had in 1913.

But what if inflation were zero? And what if you invested your one dollar, in 1913, at the same 3.10% interest? Where would you be in 2020? You'd have $26.32. But since the purchasing power of the dollar has not changed, you would have 26 times the purchasing power you had in 1913. In other words, you would be 26 times as wealthy without inflation as you would have been with inflation.

Let's put it in practical terms. In 1913 you could purchase one shirt with one dollar. With 3.10% inflation, in 2020 you would pay $26.32 to purchase the same shirt. Without inflation, in 2020 you could purchase 26 shirts with your $26.32 and have change left over, sales taxes notwithstanding.

Some people might argue that the previous calculation ignores the inflation premium that is theoretically built into interest rates. I would have to ask "what inflation premium?" Right now in the

U.S., the rate of inflation is between 3.0% and 8.0%, depending on whose numbers you believe. Even 5-year certificates of deposit don't pay enough interest to offset inflation.

If you have no savings, but a lot of debt, inflation can make it easier to pay off debt. Those $500 monthly mortgage payments you make on the note you signed 20 years ago look sweet compared to the $1,500 you'd be paying in rent now for the same house if you hadn't purchased it years ago.

Let's go back to the theory that as long as salaries and wages increase at the same rate as inflation — and assuming that all savings earn enough interest to keep up with inflation — then inflation has no negative effect. This is theoretically correct. It is also theoretically correct that if I lose two pounds a week for the next 15 weeks I'll be back down to my high school surfing weight. But theory and reality are two different things.

When the Federal Reserve creates new money, inflation will not result until the money is spent in the economy. This means that the people who get their hands on the new money first can spend it before it loses value through inflation. Who gets it first? The government. Banks. Wall Street. Big Business. By the time the money gets down to you and me, it has already been circulating in the economy and has lost part of its value through inflation.

Whether you believe the government's inflation index or some other index, and whether you think wages have stagnated since the 1970's or have kept up with inflation, one thing for certain is that the cash in your wallet or buried in your back yard is losing purchasing power daily. Inflation is waging a war on cash.

CHAPTER 10

Hiding Inflation

AS WE NOTED IN the previous chapter, the US Dollar has lost about 96% of its purchasing power since 1913. Yet we have much more comfortable lifestyles now than we did 100 years ago and can afford many more consumer goods. Almost everyone has a car and a computer and a television, etc. How is this possible?

It is possible partly because American businesses and workers have become so much more productive, and partly because of cheap foreign and imported labor. Through modern technology, workers can produce a more output with less input. This keeps prices down. For many (perhaps most) goods, the percentage of increase in worker productivity along with the use of cheaper labor has outpaced the rate of currency inflation. In effect, it hides the inflation.

Imagine how much better off we'd be if there had been no inflation. It is hard to contemplate.

Remember how much a personal computer cost in 1985? A top-of-the-line computer, like the IBM PC AT, might have cost $4,000 to $6,000 and had up to 512 megabytes of memory and a 30 megabyte hard drive. You couldn't run a smart phone with such little memory and disk space.

An average desktop computer today might cost $600 and come with a terabyte hard drive and 8 gigabytes of memory. Technology, productivity improvements, and cheaper labor dropped the price from $6,000 to $600 while increasing performance astronomically.

What if there had been no improvements in technology and worker productivity? What would that same IBM PC AT cost in today's dollars? The answer is that the $6,000 computer would cost over $14,000 in today's dollars.

When I was in college in 1990, my father bought me an AST Bravo 286 computer with 512 mb of memory and a 30 megabyte hard drive for $1,800. It had an amber monitor (no Windows and no color display). It was an average computer for that time. In today's dollars, that same computer would cost $3,258. But because of improvements in technology, science and industry has provided more computing power for less money even in the face of relentless inflation. I am typing this book on an HP desktop computer with 12 gigabytes of memory and one terabyte of hard disk space. I paid about $750 for it, which would equate to about $380 in 1990. The reduction in price between the IBM PC AT in 1990 and today's desktop with far more memory, disk space, and processing power is entirely due to improvements in technology, worker productivity, and the use of cheap foreign labor. A top-of-the-line gaming computer can be purchased today for $1,800. The effects of inflation are hidden and overwhelmed by technology and cheap labor. The government loves this because it allows them to more easily get away with creating inflation.

CHAPTER 11

Theft By Confiscation: Civil Asset Forfeiture

G OVERNMENT LOGIC: CRIMINALS OFTEN conduct business in cash in order to avoid taxes and to avoid leaving a paper trail of their transactions. Therefore, anyone who conducts transactions with cash is probably a criminal.

Using that same logic, we could say that criminals often use a car to help them commit their evil deeds. Therefore, anyone who uses a car is probably a criminal.

Governments — federal, state and local — now have a powerful tactic. Since law enforcement is often frustrated by its inability to gather enough evidence to convict someone of a crime, they have decided to make it legal to simply confiscate all the cash carried by someone they suspect might have obtained the cash by illegal means, without needing evidence of any kind.

Modern asset forfeiture law has been evolving since 1970 and has its origins in the Racketeer Influenced and Corrupt

Organization (RICO) Act of 1970, the Controlled Substances Act of 1970, and the Comprehensive Crime Control Act which took effect in 1986 under the Reagan Administration.

In addition to a myriad of state and local laws too numerous to list, civil asset forfeiture is given its teeth by the Controlled Substances Act (21 U.S.C. Sec. 881(a)(6).) The Justice Department has authorized the IRS to get in on the act.[11.1] Section 881 is not brief enough in its expression to allow me to reproduce it entirely here, so I'll give you the "sound bite" version. The full text is online. Subsection (a) has eleven paragraphs detailing what property can be seized by a suspicious law enforcement officer. I'll summarize the substance of the eleven paragraphs here:

The following items used to manufacture, transport, hide, etc., or otherwise facilitate the trafficking of controlled substances "shall be subject to forfeiture to the United States and no property right shall exist in them." (Sounds almost biblical, doesn't it?)

All controlled substances, raw materials, and equipment used to make, transport, or deliver said substances; all property used to contain such controlled substances; all vehicles used to transport controlled substances; all books and records and research; all "moneys, negotiable instruments, securities, or other things of value furnished or intended to be furnished by any person in exchange for a controlled substance or listed chemical in violation of this subchapter, all proceeds traceable to such an exchange, and all moneys, negotiable instruments, and securities used or intended to be used to facilitate any violation of this subchapter; real property, chemicals, drug paraphernalia or firearms.[11.2]

So, they can seize pretty much anything they want to. But they have to have probable cause, or reasonable suspicion, or something, right?

Simply the possession of a "large amount" of cash is enough to provide a "reasonable suspicion" to everyday law enforcement that you have either committed a crime or are planning to. As with many questionable uses of force, the confiscation of cash from "suspects" has its roots in the long and violent drug war. Remember Nancy Reagan's "just say no" campaign against drugs in the 1980's? Well now it's "just say no" to carrying too much cash, lest you look like a drug dealer or terrorist. After all, what else could you be carrying a lot of cash for, other than to buy drugs or bombs?

Think you could never be affected by this since "you've done nothing wrong?"

Perhaps you're a 31-year-old man like Matt Lee, who had trouble finding a job and was living with his parents in Michigan after losing the job that helped him keep his head above water.[11.3] When a friend arranged for a promising job interview out in California, he loaded what he could into his 14-year-old Bonneville and hit the road with $700 he'd saved up from doing odd jobs — and $2,500 his dad slipped to him in an envelope before he left.

It was an uneventful trip until he passed a couple of police officers parked on the side of a desert highway in Humboldt County, Nevada. One of the police cars took up behind Matt and pulled him over, never giving a reason why. Matt answered a barrage of questions until the officer finally got around to asking how much cash he was carrying and demanded to search his car. Feeling a bit isolated and at the mercy of the officers, he complied, hoping they would see he had nothing illegal and would let him go.

Ultimately they accused Matt of driving to California to buy drugs and they confiscated his money. This after searching his car inside and out and using a drug-detecting dog, which found no drugs. Matt had never before been in trouble with the law and did nothing to draw the attention of the police. He figured "Hey, I've got nothing to hide, so I've got nothing to fear from the police." He was wrong.

Or perhaps you're like the man in "United States vs. $133,420 in US Currency and Damon J. Louis" in San Francisco, California.[11.4] As he was driving back to San Francisco after attending a friend's wedding in Albuquerque, Mr. Louis was pulled over by an

Arizona law enforcement officer for "failing to use his turn signal." Upon questioning, Louis said there was nothing illegal in the car and denied that he was carrying a large amount of cash. The officer brought out the dog, which naturally "alerted" to something, giving the officer "probably cause" to search the vehicle. The officer found no drugs or any other contraband, but discovered over $133,000 cash in a box in the trunk.

Even though no drugs were found, the officer "arrested" the cash under suspicion that it was associated with illicit drug transactions. At trial, Louis asserted that the cash belonged to him, but refused to provide evidence as to where it came from. The court demanded that Louis produce minute detail regarding how he came to be in possession of the cash. To wit:

It was demanded that Louis supply the date(s), time, place and manner that he obtained the currency, including the names address and telephone numbers of the person(s) from whom the currency was obtained. He was to explain the circumstances of each transaction by which he acquired or obtained any interest in the currency, and he was expected to give the reason he obtained the money and to provide contact information of anyone who was a witness to the transaction(s). He was also to produce each and every document evidencing, recording, facilitating, or otherwise relating to any transaction that resulted in him acquiring the money.

Naturally, Louis refused to provide any information, saying that it was his money and was in his possession and that he wanted it returned. The court, in a circuitous Mobius strip-like self-serving opinion argued that if you can't or won't prove where your money came from, then it doesn't belong to you. It belongs to the state.

Let let that sink in.

Any law enforcement officer can pull anyone over for the tiniest infraction, commence an interrogation, then bring out the dog which will naturally alert to "drugs" anytime prompted by the officer, thus providing cover for what otherwise would be an illegal search. The officer could then confiscate any cash the person has and force the person to go before a judge to provide documentation and witnesses as to where the cash came from.

Before you rush to judgement and say that the search was justified because the dog alerted to drugs (which were not found), you should know that a high percentage of US currency is contaminated with cocaine residue. The courts acknowledge this.

In one 1985 study done by the U.S. Drug Enforcement Administration (DEA) on the money machines in a U.S. Federal Reserve district bank, random samples of $50 and $100 bills revealed that a third to a half of all the currency tested bore traces of cocaine. It's even higher than that in inner cities. Other studies have concluded similarly, including studies in Los Angeles and Miami that concluded that over ninety percent of cash in those cities was contaminated by the residue of controlled substances, particularly cocaine, which is particularly "adhesive" to cash.[11.5]

Not all asset seizures involve people secretly carrying money in their cars. Two of the most recent incidents in the news occurred at airports. The stories I'm about to relate should infuriate anyone with a pulse.

In August of 2019, Rebecca Brown of Lowell, Massachusetts was visiting her 79-year-old father, Terry Rolin, near Pittsburgh for the weekend. A retired railroad engineer who was raised by depression-era parents to distrust banks, he had squirreled away over $80,000 in cash. During the visit he agreed that since he had recently moved from a large house into an apartment, he would be more comfortable if the money was in the bank. Rebecca had to fly back home, but the banks were closed. She did an internet research to make sure it was okay to carry a large amount of cash on a domestic flight and learned that it was entirely legal. At the airport, the money attracted the attention of the TSA agent when it showed up on their X-ray screening device. She was interviewed by the TSA agent and a Pennsylvania State trooper, who finally said she was free to go and could take her cash. But before she could board the plane, the same state trooper showed up with a DEA officer in tow. The DEA agent seized the cash. Rebecca was not arrested and has not been charged with a crime. The government told Rebecca and her father that it intends to keep the money under the civil forfeiture laws. Terry and Rebecca teamed up with the Institute for Justice and sued for the return of the money. They are also filing a class action lawsuit against both DEA and TSA for taking actions that are outside their legal authority and violate the Constitution. They are also suing the individual DEA agent for damages for violating their rights.[11.6] As of March 4, 2020 the DEA has agreed to return the $82,373 it seized from Rebecca at the airport. However, the class action lawsuit will continue.[11.7]

According to the Justice Department Office of Inspector General, the DEA seized more than $4 billion in cash from people suspected of drug activity between 2007 and 2016. But $3.2 billion of the seized money never resulted in any criminal charges. Most DEA seizures happen in airports, train stations and bus terminals.[11.8]

In September 2019, a Florida trucking company, FGL Transport, Inc., gave employee Boris Nulman $191,500 in cash along with a plane ticket to Cleveland to purchase several big trucks. The TSA discovered the cash and confiscated all but $10,000. The TSA agent provided a receipt to Nulman to show that $159,950 was confiscated — $21,550 less than what the trucking company says was seized. The company has evidence to show the money came from its business account. A Customs official claimed, without providing evidence, that the money was proceeds from unlawful activity. The company and its owners are filing a lawsuit to have the money returned.[11.9] According to the lawsuit, buying used big rigs from owner-operators for cash is a common practice.

Civil Asset Forfeiture is yet another government policy that may have been born of good intentions and may be necessary in some cases, but is suffering from serious abuse in the hands of federal, state, and local law enforcement agencies. Despite many attempts to rein in the abuses, the preceding events make it clear that the clear violation of constitutionally protected rights continues.

Civil asset forfeiture is no joke, but if you prefer a sugar-coating of humor on explanations of controversial issues, John Oliver does a great job of entertaining while horrifying his audience with the realities of civil asset forfeiture in a 16 minute video.[11.10]

CHAPTER 12

The Four-legged Search Warrant

DESPITE THE WIDESPREAD CONTAMINATION of cash with drug residue, detection dogs are still used. Though a positive alert by a dog is not supposed to be enough to provide probable cause for an arrest, it is very effective in neutralizing the Fourth Amendment prohibition of unreasonable searches.

For an enlightening discussion of dog vs. cash we turn to a 1994 case heard by the United States Court of Appeals for the Ninth Circuit: United States v. $30,060 US Currency and Albert Joseph Alexander.[12.1] It seems that Mr. Alexander was stopped by the Los Angeles County Sherriff's Department for running a stop sign. During the stop the deputy noticed a bag on the front seat containing about $30,000 in cash, in neat bundles of $1,000. As usual, a dog alerted to the smell of drugs, and even though no drugs were found in the car, the cash was confiscated on suspicion of being used in the drug trade.

Alexander was not arrested, nor was he charged with a crime. There was no evidence that he committed a crime, and the question before the court was not whether Alexander committed a crime. The question before the court was whether the cash was connected to drugs. To confiscate the cash, the government must demonstrate that there was probable cause to do so. The judge cited a prior case where the court articulated that probable cause is based on "the aggregate of facts" and "simply involves the question whether the information relied on by the government is adequate and sufficiently reliable to warrant the belief by a reasonable person that the [money] was" connected to drugs." Citing another case, the judge wrote: "To pass the point of mere suspicion and to reach probable cause, it is necessary to demonstrate by some credible evidence the probability that the money was in fact connected to drugs."

"Some credible evidence."

Does a trained dog's alert amount to credible evidence that the money was connected to drugs? Considering that most currency has drug residue on it, it would not seem so.

The judge observed that in the past, his court had indeed ruled that an alert by a trained dog was "strong evidence" when making a probable cause determination, but he then added that "In recent years . . . subsequent courts, including our own, have questioned the probative value of positive dog alerts due to the contamination of America's paper money supply with narcotics residue."

The judge then cited numerous cases that refused to rely solely on the dog's nose to demonstrate probable cause. The judge devoted several paragraphs showing that a dog can find drug residue on almost anyone's money, citing authoritative study after study over a period of years, finally concluding with this:

"Undoubtedly, a positive dog alert is probative in showing that the currency has been in contact with a narcotics substance or contaminated currency at some 'prior' point in time. Dickerson, 873 F.2d at 1184. The mere fact of prior contamination does not establish, however, that the currency was actually exchanged for or intended to be exchanged for drugs by the person currently in possession of the currency — especially when seventy-five percent of Los Angeles' paper money supply is tainted with drug residue." The court did recognize that cash that contained a larger amount of drug residue than would normally be found on the average Federal Reserve Note might be a more suspicious.

What other sort of evidence, other than the dog's nose, might be needed to support probable cause? The judge in the Alexander case cites another cash confiscation case where the money was carried on a flight to a known drug-source city. The money was concealed and strapped to the suspect's body, and the travel agency that issued the suspect's ticket was known to have issued tickets to 20-30 other people from whom the police had seized narcotics-related currency. Such things don't look good on any resume other than that of a drug dealer. But in Alexander's case, no such circumstances were in evidence.

The court ruled that Alexander's $30,060 in cash had to be returned to Alexander as the dog's faithful nose was not enough to show probable cause that the cash was guilty, and the fact that Alexander lied about his employment status and appeared not to have a regular source of income were not sufficient evidence to show that the money was obtained by Alexander through the drug trade.

But not all the judges deciding the case agreed. The judge who wrote the dissenting opinion basically said "Oh, come on, where else would an unemployed loser get $30,000 in cash other than by dealing drugs. Everybody knows he has to be guilty." Right. Who needs evidence when it's so obvious?

Fortunately, the majority opined in favor of Alexander, and he got his money back. And the dog's nose theoretically diminished in importance.

In April 2015 the US Supreme Court has handed down a decision that further affects the use of a dog's nose.[122] This decision regards the use of a drug -detecting dog in a routine traffic stop in Nebraska. In March 2012, a law enforcement officer observed a vehicle veer briefly onto the shoulder of the road. He pulled the vehicle over. Inside was Dennys Rodriguez and passenger. Rodriguez explained to the officer that he veered onto the shoulder to avoid a pothole. Since driving on the shoulder is illegal, the officer issued Rodriguez a ticket. After concluding the traffic stop, the officer requested permission to allow his drug dog to sniff around the Rodriguez's vehicle. Rodriguez denied permission. The officer called for backup and extended the traffic stop by "seven or eight minutes" to wait for backup. The officer searched without permission and the dog found drugs (meth) in the vehicle.

At trial, the District Court judge agreed that the officer had no probable cause (other than the dog alert) to search Rodriguez's vehicle, *but* since the search only took eight minutes, it was not sufficiently intrusive to violate Rodriguez's Fourth Amendment rights and was therefore permissible. The Eighth Circuit Court of Appeals agreed with the District Court. This is bizarre reasoning. Essentially, what the courts are saying is that it's okay to conduct an illegal search if done quickly enough so that the suspect is not unreasonably inconvenienced.

Fortunately, the US Supreme Court easily saw through this faulty analysis and held that "absent reasonable suspicion, police extension of a traffic stop in order to conduct a dog sniff violates the Constitution's shield against unreasonable seizures." The Supreme Court said that during a traffic stop, ". . . an officer's mission typically includes ". . . checking the driver's license, determining whether there are outstanding warrants against the driver, and inspecting the automobile's registration and proof of insurance." And that "lacking the same close connection to roadway safety as the ordinary inquiries, a dog sniff is not fairly characterized as part of the officer's traffic mission." The Supreme Court sent the case back to the lower court for reconsideration, because the question remains as to whether reasonable suspicion of criminal activity justified detaining Rodriguez beyond completion of the traffic infraction investigation. To be clear (if you're still trying to make sense of this case) the Supreme Court only ruled that an officer cannot extend an ordinary traffic stop to conduct a dog sniff of the vehicle if there is no reasonable suspicion.

So, for instance, if you have a large envelope on the front seat with one hundred dollar bills falling out of it, the officer might (I'm not a lawyer) have reasonable suspicion or even probable cause sufficient to extend a routine traffic stop to conduct a dog sniff.

The Rodriguez Case is interesting, and I recommend you read it: Rodriguez v. United States 741 F. 3d 905, vacated and remanded. The opinion was written by Ruth Bader Ginsberg. There were three dissenting judges: Kennedy, Thomas, and Alito. Reading the published dissents offers a window into the thinking of the conservative judiciary that allows leeway toward incursion on natural rights when it comes to possible drug offenses. Thomas quotes from a precedent case which, when probable cause is lacking, prescribes comparing the degree to which a search intrudes on an individual's right to privacy against the degree to which the search is needed for the promotion of legitimate governmental interests. This is the type of incrementally progressive reinterpretation of the delegated powers of the Constitution, a reinterpretation that allows the *de facto* destruction of the Constitution by broad interpretations of the "general welfare" and "regulation of interstate commerce" clauses in Article 1, Section 8, which clauses are now used to justify any action by the federal government.

The effect of this suspicion toward citizens who are lawfully carrying significant amounts of cash is to instill fear — to gradually create an environment where anyone carrying a roll of cash is suspect. It's working. Who wants to risk being caught with a significant amount of hard-earned cash and risk losing it?

CHAPTER 13

Your Bank Teller Is Spying on You

BANKS AROUND THE WORLD are adopting invasive surveillance methods. Dr. Anthony Daniels, a well-known retired British doctor who writes insightful analysis and commentary under the pseudonym Theodore Dalrymple, received an email from his British bank's "business standards officer" regarding his US dollar account. The email asked "Can you please confirm the source of funds . . . which have been deposited in your account? If these funds are work-related can you please confirm the nature of your work, who your employers are and if you anticipate this to continue? Can you please advise why the funds are paid to your international account, rather than being paid to your UK account?" Dr. Daniel was asked to provide all that information within 14 days.[13.1]

Daniels was surprised because he thought that his private business was, well, his private business. He had been a customer of the bank for nearly fifty years and it was perfectly obvious from the checks and direct transfers into his account what the source of the funds was. Upon inquiry, Daniels was told the email query was "to comply with legislation and . . . to reduce fraud, identity theft and financial crime by maintaining accurate and secure records." Of course Daniels did not miss the irony presented by the facts: his bank ". . . has repeatedly been forced to admit that it has engaged on huge-scale dishonesty that has cost it billions in fines and reparations."

The lesson that Dr. Daniels took from his banking experience was that ". . . privacy no longer exists, that everyone is presumed guilty by government or bank until proven innocent, and that the ordinary citizen may be intimidated, misled and lied to without shame."

You're likely to find yourself in trouble if you do any of the following on a regular basis:

- Deposit significant amounts of cash in your bank account.

- Withdraw significant amounts of cash from your bank account.

- Purchase expensive items with cash.

- Carry large amounts of cash (more than perhaps $1,000 or so; who knows?).

But how does the government know how much cash you're withdrawing or depositing and how often you do it? As we've seen earlier in our discussion of Operation Choke Point, the government employs financial services firms like banks to keep an eye on their customers. Banks are required to report certain cash transactions to the government or face serious repercussions. Your bank teller is spying on you.

A bank has to file a Currency Transaction Report (CTR) for every transaction in currency that is more than $10,000.[13.2] "Transaction" means deposits, withdrawals, exchanges, or other payments or transfers by, through, or to the bank. Here are a few types of transaction this cash reporting rule would apply to:

- IRA deposits
- Loan payments
- ATM transactions
- Certificate of Deposit purchases
- Deposits and withdrawals
- Currency exchanges, and more.

What is "currency?" Currency is defined as coin and paper money of the United States or any other country. In other words, cash and coins.

But it isn't just the bank that's spying on you. Merchants, including car dealers also have to file a CTR if a customer pays with cash of more than $10,000. So if you paid a car dealer $10,001 cash for a car, the dealer would have to notify the government by filing a CTR to report the transaction and your identifying information.

Don't think you can get around the reporting requirement by making multiple transactions, each below $10,000. Financial institutions are required to aggregate all cash transactions from one person in one business day. Banks are given considerable power and responsibility in reporting cash transactions. For instance, what if one person owns multiple corporations? Are the corporations treated separately? Or are all cash transactions of each corporation aggregated each business day?

According to the Federal Financial Institutions Examination Council, ". . . if the bank accounts of one business are repeatedly used to pay the expenses of another business, or the business bank accounts are repeatedly used to pay the personal expenses of the owner, the financial institution may determine that aggregating the businesses' [cash] transactions is appropriate because the transactions were made on behalf of a single person."

Did you get that? The bank is given the power to determine if your corporation is paying any of your personal expenses. Banks are instructed to make a judgement as to whether a person's various businesses are operating independently, whether they're co-mingling cash, or are by some other evidence available to the bank, not operating "separately or independently of one another or their common owner." Businesses and owners that are judged by the bank to not be operating independently are to have their daily cash transactions aggregated and reported on a CTR when the $10,000 transaction is met.[13.3] Presumably cash transactions falling under, but close to the $10,000 threshold could be reported as "structuring." That's invasive monitoring. Based on my interactions with bank tellers and managers, I'm not sure they are qualified to make those judgements.

Even if you don't have an account relationship with a particular institution, it still has to collect personal information from you, such as your Social Security number or driver's license number if you engage in a cash transaction in excess of $10,000. My experience has been that trying to cash a check — even for $500 — at a bank where one does not have an account will result in a demand for one's Social Security Number, Driver's License, a description of one's employment, and in many cases, a fingerprint (on a conveniently provided ink pad). Though smiling broadly, they treat you like a suspected criminal. A FinCEN information pamphlet says this: "The financial institution collects this information in a manner consistent with a customer's right to financial privacy." That's about as meaningful as a cop that performed an illegal search telling the judge that the search was conducted in a manner consistent with the suspect's right to be free from unreasonable searches and seizures. Only a government can get away with writing contradictory gibberish like that.

A U.S. financial institution has to file a CTR within 15 days of a transaction and must retain copies of CTRs for five years. The reports are filed with the Financial Crimes Enforcement Network (FinCEN) which is part of the U.S. Treasury.

The CTR law is so draconian that, even if you're not engaged in money laundering, drug trafficking or any other crime, you can still be imprisoned for up to five years and fined up to $500,000 for trying to avoid having your cash transactions reported to the government by making a series of small deposits that add up to $10,000 or more. The government has a word for this: "structuring."

The CTR is not the only method financial institutions have of reporting you to the government. Another reporting mechanism is called the Suspicious Activity Report (SAR). It can be triggered by any activity that appears "suspicious." Although it can be triggered by non-financial activity, cash transactions of $5,000 or more that seem as though they may be tied to some possible illegal activity can result in the bank filing an SAR. Just inquiring about whether a transaction you're about to conduct will generate a CTR may be enough to trigger the filing of an SAR.

Many banks have been convicted of fraud,[13.4] collusion,[13.5] and money laundering[13.5] on a scale so massive as to be inconceivable to the average person. It is intolerably ironic that these same banks are charged with monitoring, harassing, and destroying small businesses and individuals who unknowingly fall afoul of a technical mousetrap regulation or attempt to make a living doing something that some political overlord frowns upon.

CHAPTER 14

Structuring: The Crime of . . .

STRUCTURING TRANSACTIONS IS A crime by itself, even if you're not committing any other crime. Let me be clear: the IRS and Department of Justice considers a series of deposits or withdrawals, each under $10,000 but adding up to more than $10,000 in total, to be sufficient evidence of structuring to confiscate money in the accounts involved, without any other evidence of wrongdoing. Following are four examples of illegally structured transactions as given in a Financial Crimes Enforcement Network (FinCEN) educational pamphlet.[14.1] Only the last example involves money laundering. The others are just ordinary people who'd rather not have their private activities reported to the government:

1. John has $15,000 in cash obtained from selling his truck. John knows that if he deposits $15,000 in cash, his financial

institution will be required to file a Currency Transaction Report (CTR). John instead deposits $7,500 in cash in the morning with one financial institution employee and comes back to the financial institution later in the day to another employee to deposit the remaining $7,500, hoping to evade the CTR reporting requirement.

2. Jane needs $18,000 in cash to pay for supplies for her wood carving business. Jane cashes a $9,000 personal check at a financial institution on a Monday, then cashes another $9,000 personal check at the financial institution the following day. Jane cashed the checks separately and structured the transactions in an attempt to evade the CTR reporting requirement.

3. A married couple, John and Jane, sell a vehicle for $15,000 in cash. To evade the CTR reporting requirement, John and Jane structure their transactions using different accounts. John deposits $8,000 of that money into his and Jane's joint account in the morning. Later that day, Jane deposits $1,500 into the joint account, and then $5,500 into her sister's account, which is later transferred to John and Jane's joint account.

4. Bob wants to place $24,000 cash he earned from his illegal activities into the financial system by using a wire transfer. Bob knows his financial institution will file a CTR if he purchases a wire with over $10,000 currency in one day. To evade the CTR reporting requirement, Bob wires the $24,000 by purchasing wires with currency in $6,000 increments over a short period of time, occasionally skipping days in an attempt to prevent the financial institution from filing a CTR.

Notice how FinCEN equates ordinary people, like John and Jane, who are simply managing their legally earned money, with Bob, who earned money from his illegal activities. The government is clearly denying honest people their privacy and the right to be secure in their papers. I'm sure I recall reading these words somewhere in the U.S. Constitution: "The right of the people to be secure in their persons, houses, papers, and effects, against unreasonable searches and seizures, shall not be violated . . ." Perhaps that was the Fourth Amendment. Check your copy of the Constitution.

Some people will say "so what?" If you aren't doing anything wrong, why do you care if your transaction is reported to the IRS or any other governmental agency? Why try to hide your cash transactions?

Maybe you aren't trying to hide. Maybe the bank just thinks you are.

Three common reasons people may keep their transactions under $10,000:

1. They don't know it's a crime to do so.

2. Their business insurance does not cover cash losses greater than $10,000, so if an employee gets robbed on the way to the bank with more than $10,000, it's not insured.

3. They may have been advised by colleagues or bank employees, or even their CPA, that keeping their deposits below $10,000 saves the bank paperwork.[14.2]

Carole Hinders of Arnolds Park, Iowa owned a Mexican restaurant for nearly 40 years. Her restaurant did not accept credit cards or debit cards. Cash only. Naturally, she made significant cash deposits on a daily basis, all under $10,000. The bank reported her for "structuring" and the IRS seized her checking account with over $30,000 in it.[14.3] She had done nothing "wrong." But it didn't matter. To keep her business going she's had to mortgage her house.

Ms. Hinders was not being charged with money laundering or with failing to pay taxes on the money. She was guilty only of depositing less than $10,000 at a time.

For a year and a half, Ms. Hinders lived at the intersection of Structuring Avenue and Civil Asset Forfeiture Boulevard. The burden was on her to prove she was not deliberately structuring. (The IRS agreed to return her money and the case was dismissed "without prejudice," which means the IRS can still go after that money again in the future.)[14.4] In a way, Hinders was innocently structuring. She had once been told that if you include more than $10,000 in one deposit, the bank has to do a lot of paperwork. She thought she was saving the bank the trouble of doing the paperwork.

You laugh. How naïve of Ms. Hinders. Banks love paperwork. Right?

Bi-County Distributors, a Long Island, NY company made frequent cash deposits and had several of its bank accounts closed over the years because the bank got tired of the paperwork burden of filing all those CTRs. On the (bad) advice of their accountant, they started keeping their deposits under $10,000 to avoid having their accounts closed. The Justice Department seized over $400,000 of their account balances. Although the company and its owners have not been charged with a crime, the DOJ intended to keep the money. But the Institute for Justice helped them file a lawsuit which created a lot of negative publicity for the IRS, which notified the company's owners in January 2015 that it would return their money, three years after seizing it.[14.5]

Ironically, sometimes bank tellers advise businesses to keep deposits under $10,000 to avoid the reporting requirement. South Mountain Creamery in Middletown, MD did just that on the advice of a bank teller: the IRS seized $67,000 of their money, of which the IRS got to keep $29,000.[14.6]

In the gun sales boom in the wake of Sandy Hook gun control legislation, Clyde Armory in Athens, Georgia did $1.2 million in cash sales in a few months. Because the store's insurance policy only covered cash losses of $10,000 or less outside of the store, the Armory never transported more than $10,000 at one time to the bank. The IRS seized almost one million dollars from the Armory's account and threatened the owner with a felony for depositing his own legally earned cash.[147] The owner ended up settling for $50,000 just to get his money back. This is legalized governmental extortion. This is the same government that tells us that it's empowered to look out for "the general welfare" of the people.

These individuals and business owners thought they were doing nothing wrong and didn't think they had any reason to hide anything or fear the government. They were wrong. Fortunately, this outrageous abuse of power resulted in Congressional hearings, which caused the IRS to back off. On October 17, 2014, Richard Weber, Chief of IRS Criminal Investigation, announced that it would no longer seize cash from businesses that were suspected only of structuring (legal source structuring) without any other criminal activity (illegal source structuring).[148]

Unfortunately, the IRS's new policy has enough vague language to continue to accommodate whatever enforcement action the government wishes to take. Specifically, they'll still seize the funds if there are "exceptional circumstances justifying the seizure and forfeiture and the case has been approved at the director of field operations level."

In the wake of the moderating stance supposedly taken by the IRS in October 2014, Eric Holder's Justice Department issued Policy Directive 15-3 on March 31, 2015, stating that, in light of its own review of forfeiture in structuring cases as well as its review of the IRS's new policy, the Justice Department would henceforth only seize structured funds when there'a probable cause that the funds were generated by unlawful activity or intended to be used in unlawful activity.[149]

If the IRS and the Justice Department do follow their new policy and don't abuse the loopholes, relief for honest people might result. But what about the many cases currently being litigated? Will the government back off in light of the new policies?

Janet Malone, a 68-year-old widow from Dubuque, Iowa has been charged with structuring and has had $19,000 seized from her bank account by the IRS.[14.10] It is a case where no crime was committed other than making a series of cash deposits in increments less than $10,000. Malone's husband was dying of cancer. In 2011, he made a series of cash deposits totaling $35,000. The IRS investigated, even visiting Ronald Malone at his home and warned him about the structuring law, going so far as to make him sign a form acknowledging that he'd been warned that the deposits could appear to be structured.

Before he passed away, Ronald Malone told his wife, Janet, about a briefcase he had with $180,000 cash from his job, his gambling winnings, and some investment income. After his death, she began depositing the cash in increments of less than $10,000. In 2015, the IRS seized $19,000 that she had deposited and charged her with structuring. She faced a $250,000 fine and up to a year in jail. Sixty eight years old, she just lost her husband, and the government wants to lock her up because she deposited her own legally earned cash in the bank. She pled guilty to avoid jail. U.S. Magistrate Judge Jon Scoles sentenced her to forfeit the $19,000, pay a $2,500 fine, and serve one year of probation.[14.11]

Lyndon McLellan, like his parents before him, owned a country store in North Carolina. L&M Convenience Mart is a convenience store with a gas station. It also has a restaurant with hot dogs, hamburgers, and catfish sandwiches on the menu. In July 2014, more than a dozen federal agents, including the FBI, entered his business. Agents accused him of structuring, because he had a history of making cash deposits of less than $10,000. They informed him that the IRS had seized his entire bank account balance of $107,702.66. Although Mr. McLellan had never heard of "structuring" and didn't handle his store's bank deposits himself, his niece, who handled the deposits was following a bank teller's instructions to keep deposits below $10,000 so the bank would not have to do extra paperwork (Currency Transaction Reports).[14.12]

But what about the IRS's new policy of only pursuing structuring seizures where the money was obtained through illegal activities?

"During a February 2015 [House Ways and Means Oversight Subcommittee] hearing on civil asset forfeiture, IRS Commissioner John Koskinen was asked broadly about McLellan's case, in which there were no criminal charges pending or illegal activity conducted." Koskinen's response was 'If that case exists, then it's not following the policy.'"[14.13]

The government offered to give Mr. McLellan half of his money back if he agreed to a settlement by March 30, 2015. He refused the offer. Since then, the government has dropped the structuring charges against McLellan citing the new policy of the Justice Department. The government has agreed to return all of the money, but wants to keep the interest. The Institute for Justice is representing McLellan and is helping to recover his money and legal expenses.[14.14] Ultimately, in the face of public outrage, the government decided to dismiss the case against McLellan, but refused to cover his legal fees of more than $20,000 even though he is entitled to reimbursement.[14.15]

While the Justice Departments new policy seems to offer some relief, the directive has a wide loophole and an exception. The loophole is that if an "investigation" cannot determine the source of the funds, they are presumed to be from an unlawful source. The exception is that regardless of the statement that only unlawfully sourced funds will be seized, permission may be obtained from a U.S. Attorney or from the Chief of the Asset Forfeiture and Money Laundering Section to seize any funds suspected of being structured.[14.16]

But how big of a problem is this? How much cash has been seized? Surely only a few people have been affected, and this has been blown way out of proportion by a few libertarian anti-government sovereign citizen types, right? Is this yet another conspiracy theory?

The Institute for Justice, a nonprofit organization that specializes in monitoring and challenging civil asset forfeitures, obtained

IRS data that showed "from 2005 to 2012, the IRS seized more than $242 million for suspected structuring violations in more than 2,500 cases . . . [At] least a third of those cases arose from nothing more than a series of cash transactions under $10,000 with no other criminal activity alleged." On average, it takes a year to recover the money seized. The fact that nearly half of the $242 million eventually had to be returned is evidence that's seizing much more than can be justified.[14.17]

In July 2019, President Donald J. Trump signed the Taxpayer First Act which codifies the previous shift in IRS policy of not seizing cash unconnected to criminal activity other than structuring. Unfortunately, the restrictions in the new law do not apply to the Department of Justice. Institute for Justice Senior Attorney Darpana Sheth remarked that this is ". . . the first time in nearly two decades that Congress has reined in federal forfeiture laws, and is an important first step in addressing one type of forfeiture abuse by one federal agency. But civil forfeiture by other agencies continues unabated."[14.18]

Forfeiture is an issue that transcends party lines. Forfeiture reform bills continue to be introduced into Congress. The Institute for Justice reports that in February 2019 the U.S. Supreme Court unanimously decided that state civil forfeiture cases are bound by the Eighth Amendment's ban on "excessive fines," and that in the past five years, 33 states and D.C. have enacted forfeiture reforms.[14.19]

If I were to write an "executive summary" of this chapter, it might look like this:

Depositing or withdrawing cash in amounts of more than $10,000 is viewed as suspicious and must be reported by banks to the government. Also, multiple small deposits or withdrawals of cash in amounts of $10,000 or less but totaling more than $10,000 is suspicious and must be reported by banks to the government. The Banking Secrecy Act was intended to combat criminal activity, not to turn legitimate transactions by ordinary citizens into criminal acts, yet that's what happened. President Trump signed the Taxpayer First Act in 2019 to stop the IRS from seizing cash that was not involved in a criminal act other than structuring. Unfortunately, this law does not apply to the Department of Justice which continues to engage in seizures merely for suspected structuring.

CHAPTER 15

The Underground Cash Economy

THE INTERNAL REVENUE SERVICE (IRS) is one of the most powerful bureaucracies in the U.S. With the passage of the Affordable Care Act (aka Obamacare), it became even more powerful. We've seen how it was able to shut a business down based on nothing more than a pattern of cash deposits or withdrawals. The tax system itself is based on the close surveillance of monetary transactions through a mandatory paper trail.

The IRS refers to our tax system as "voluntary." They even have Senator Harry Reid on their side trying to convince us that the system is entirely voluntary.[15.1] We all know that's ridiculous, but if you want to hear Reid for yourself, just go to YouTube and type the following in the YouTube search box: "Reid Taxation Is Voluntary" without the quotation marks to view the four-minute excerpt from Senator Reid's interview by Jan Helfeld.

Because taxes are "voluntary," the government needs to force everyone to pay their "fair share." So they've set up a system of reporting that employers and businesses use to let the IRS know that you've been paid in exchange for services. The IRS wants to know when you've received money, because, according to the 16th Amendment to the Constitution, Congress has the power "to lay and collect taxes on income, from whatever source derived," and it makes every effort to fully exercise that power.[15.2]

We'll now take a short and controversial detour to discuss the income tax. For the record, I'm of the opinion that the individual income tax is legal, but unconstitutional and that the 16th Amendment should be repealed. It is beyond the scope of this text to expand on the particulars, but for the curious, the following paragraphs explain the law that Congress and the IRS rely on to legitimize their authority to collect income taxes on wages and self-employment income.

In Title 26, Section 61(a), we find the definition of "gross income" as follows: " Except as otherwise provided in this subtitle, gross income means all income from whatever source derived . . ." It then goes on to list examples of types of income that are taxable.[15.3] What this means is that unless Congress rules that certain types of income are exempt from taxation, or provides deductions or credits, any money you receive is taxable. For inquiring minds, see IRC Section 61 for a list of items specifically included in gross income, and Title 26, Part III, Sections 101 through 140, for items specifically excluded from gross income (like death benefits from life insurance).[15.4]

Section 1 of the Internal Revenue Code, in a long-winded directive, with each paragraph beginning with "There is hereby imposed on the taxable income of . . ." (fill in the blank: married individual, surviving spouse, head of household, etc.) sets forth who is subject to tax and what their tax rate is.[15.5]

Section 63 of the Internal Revenue Code defines "taxable income" as ". . . gross income minus the deductions allowed. . ."[15.6]

To summarize, taxable income is gross income minus allowable deductions. The people subject to tax are defined in Section 1.

So there you have it. Despite all the heartfelt and sometimes compelling arguments of tax protesters, Congress tells us exactly what gross income is, what taxable income is, who is subject to it, and what the tax rates are. Any ambiguities — and there are many — have long since been hammered out by the courts in favor of the U.S. Treasury. Fight with the IRS at your own peril. I mean no disrespect to brave and dedicated tax protesters like Irwin Schiff, Larken Rose, Sherry Peel Jackson, Joe Banister, Aaron Russo and many others.

So how does the IRS know that you've earned "income?" The IRS keeps track of your income through a system of reports that it forces employers to file under threat of penalties. If you've ever had a job — and increasing numbers of Americans have never had that opportunity — you're familiar with IRS Form W-2. The W-2 reports all your wages to the IRS so you cannot escape taxation.

If you're not an employee, but an independent contractor (aka "freelancer"), the business that pays you has to report the payments to the IRS on a form 1099 if it pays you $600 or more during the calendar year. Your social security number is on the 1099, so the IRS easily adds up all the amounts on all the 1099's issued with your name and social security number and will expect you to report at least that much income on your tax return.

How does the IRS force businesses to issue W-2 forms and 1099 forms? It uses penalties for the W-2s, potentially high penalties. Any employer that fails to withhold from wages social security and federal income tax and deposit those taxes in a bank that accepts federal tax deposits might as well kiss their business goodbye.

For 1099 forms, the IRS also charges penalties to a business that does not issue 1099s to its independent contractors. Though it is not widely known, these penalties can be quite high if the business has a lot of independent contractors.

Once your income is reported to the IRS on a form W-2 or a form 1099, you have no choice but to report it on your tax return, assuming you meet the applicable filing thresholds. This system of reporting has worked out very well for the US Treasury, particularly the W-2 reporting system and the automatic withholding tax put in place during World War II.[15.7] As you read earlier, systems are being considered that will automatically withhold taxes from other types of transactions as well.

The IRS doesn't like businesses that accept a lot of cash and pay their contractors and vendors with it. Even when they're honest, the IRS treats them with great suspicion and assumes they're pocketing cash. If you have ever waited tables in a restaurant you know this. The IRS assumes you make a certain amount of tips in cash and the reporting mechanism for employers and tipped employees is complicated and burdensome. The IRS wants to be sure they get it all.

The IRS has special audit procedures for "cash intensive" businesses. They know how to figure out if a business is pocketing cash without reporting it to the IRS. For instance, the IRS will look at purchases of inventory. Let's say you're a hotdog vendor and the average price you sell a hotdog for is five dollars. The IRS will look to see how many hotdogs you purchased during the year. If you purchased 4,000 hot dogs and buns, the auditor will expect to see you reporting sales revenues of at least $20,000. That's 4,000 hotdogs multiplied by the five-dollar sales price. Same for anything else you sell.

Of course, everyone's heard of the lifestyle audit. People operating cash intensive businesses (legal or illegal) often get caught because they report $40,000 of income on their tax return, but they live in a $750,000 house and drive a Maserati to the marina to board their 45-foot boat. The IRS can figure this out. Unless the taxpayers can prove they won the lottery or got a big inheritance, they are in trouble.

The tax evaders who are the hardest to catch are the smaller ones — the ones who fly under the radar. The IRS refers to this as "the underground economy," made up of small, single, entrepreneurial businesses that can receive payment for their goods or services in the form of cash. This makes it easier to avoid reporting income and paying taxes to governments.

The underground economy consists of both legal and illegal business activities. It includes drug sales, money laundering, prostitution, sales of stolen merchandise, gambling, etc. But according the IRS, it also includes things like the house in your neighborhood with perpetual yard sales, eBay sellers, craft fairs, people selling homemade tamales, mechanics repairing cars in the backyard, people collecting cans and bottles for recycling, and day laborers on street corners. I know we all think those people collecting cans for recycling should definitely pay more in taxes. Other businesses the IRS has an eye out for include child care and pet sitting, car flipping, tree trimming and yard work, hauling, and small construction projects by unlicensed tradesmen.[15.8]

The IRS asserts that the underground economy entrepreneur is often actively working to maintain a low economic level that does not draw attention. Perhaps they simply have a sideline business to supplement their (taxed) day job.

If the IRS has trouble discovering all the cash transactions that take place, it's not for want of trying. They have special audit programs and employee training programs for discovering and auditing cash-intensive businesses like beauty shops, bail bonds, car washes, coin-operated amusements, convenience stores, laundromats, scrap metal, and taxicabs.

The IRS seeks to marshal support for its battle against Aunt Mary, who cuts and styles hair in her spare bedroom for extra money, by asserting that Aunt Mary unfairly competes against licensed beauty salons. Because Mary does not have a license or pay taxes, she can charge $10 for the same hair cut that normally goes for $30. I think their argument fails, because I'm a licensed Certified Public Accountant and pay taxes on my income. But I work out of my home instead of leasing an office downtown. For that reason I can charge much lower fees to my nonprofit clientele (I specialize in nonprofit tax compliance) than many of my competitors. There's no doubt that even if Mary kept her license up-to-date and paid taxes on her profits, she could still undercut the prices of her competitors who lease storefronts. Even with her lower prices, it's is unlikely that Mary can take significant business from a professional storefront beauty salon. And so what if she did? Is Mary less deserving of earning a living by using her skills to make people look better while saving them money?

Many years ago my former hair stylist, whom I met in a mall salon, was between jobs because of her family situation. My son and I went to her home several times to get our hair cut after she left the salon. She charged less than the salon. I was in college at the time, and it worked out well for me financially. I paid cash. Did she report the income to the IRS? I have no idea.

Interestingly, the IRS admits what a terrible tax burden Congress has placed on hard-working families with this statement made on a page of the irs.gov website: "An undergrounder earning $40,000 can provide his family with the same lifestyle a wage earner can provide with $60,000. As a result, with very little overhead, they can provide their services at a lower cost. This will be attractive to other entrepreneurs who need to cut costs, and in a sluggish economy, [it is also attractive] to consumers hoping to stretch their buying dollars." Of course, the IRS is doing everything possible to prevent any "dollar-stretching" by the working class. And they have studied well their adversary, the underground worker.

CHAPTER 16

IRS Profiling of the Underground Worker

THE IRS HAS IDENTIFIED traits that typical underground cash workers display, such as.[16.1] They:

+ Keep a low profile by driving an old car and living in a lower-income neighborhood so as not to draw attention.

+ Advertise through word-of-mouth or in free local papers.

+ Screen calls with an answering machine to learn more about the customer before accepting a job.

+ May use a Post Office Box to protect their personal residence from scrutiny.

+ Engage in a trade that requires minimal investment and has low overhead expenses.

+ Often won't have a bank account and, if they do, avoid depositing cash that they don't report.

- Will cash checks they receive in payment instead of depositing them in the bank.
- Seek to be paid in cash and provide a phony Social Security number when asked or make up a phony corporate name to make the business think a 1099 does not have to be issued.
- Are resourceful and on the alert for cash-earning opportunities.
- May be public assistance recipients.
- Pay living expenses with cash or money order.
- May not have business liability insurance, vehicle insurance, or worker compensation insurance. If they have helpers, the helpers will be unreported and paid in cash.
- Will own a safe.

Let's summarize the typical underground worker: they drive an old beater and live in a run-down high-crime neighborhood (or fit multiple families into a house in a nice neighborhood) and don't have a bank account. They advertise in free local papers. They're resourceful and always on the lookout for a way to provide services and earn money by charging low prices and asking to be paid with cash. They can't afford insurance. They have a safe at home because they live in a dangerous neighborhood, everyone else in the neighborhood has a cheap safe (because nobody has enough money or money management skills to maintain a bank account), and everybody knows people keep cash in the house. This definitely sounds like the type of person we need to crack down on. I'm sure if we could root out these tax cheats, we could afford to bail out the banks any time they need it without having to print money.

One technique the IRS uses to identify and expose undergrounders is to look for certain documents when they are auditing a business. If the agent encounters a handwritten invoice that was paid in cash, an underground worker may have been the recipient of that cash. The agent is trained to ask questions and to try to identify the worker.

If the agent finds the underground worker, but learns that they don't appear to be living beyond the means of their reported income, the agent is instructed not to be dissuaded. Additional investigative work is called for, which may lead to unreported cash.

Agents are taught to look for advertisements on community bulletin boards — 3x5 cards and cheap flyers. But they are especially encouraged to look for cash purchases of real estate or cars purchased from private parties with cash. It's difficult to reconcile certain aspects of the IRS internal guidance on discovering and auditing cash-intensive businesses, since the profile presented is of single-person business operating on the downlow. This is hardly indicative of a business enterprise that would generate much income. Yet, the IRS seems to think that some undergrounders are purchasing real estate in another town with cash, or spending large amounts of cash for a car. Perhaps the illegal "trades" would fall into this category. But it's hard to picture someone selling tamales out of their house or doing car repairs in the back yard being able to generate that kind of cash.

Here are some audit techniques employed by the IRS on cash-intensive businesses:

The IRS will look at the suspect's assets and interest expense. If, for instance, a shadetree mechanic purchased an expensive set of tools, but didn't incur debt to do so, the agent will suspect unreported cash income.

The IRS looks for evidence of barter activity (a painter receives a new MacBook pro in exchange for painting a computer shop).

The IRS will examine bank accounts to find where checks are written to pay the electric bill, the mortgage, the water bill, car insurance, etc. If the amount of the checks written does not equal the bills that were due, the IRS will determine that those bills were paid with unreported cash.

A new car or boat with no loans against them indicates that they may have been acquired with unreported cash.

The IRS will look for asset reports disclosed by civil, criminal, and family court proceedings (including divorces).

And of course, the IRS will not hesitate to call your neighbors, your boss, your business associates, your ex, and your creditors to see if they'll rat you out.

So, what are we to conclude from the existence of a cash-based, underground economy made up of legal (or mostly legal) business activities whose owners don't report part or all of their cash income? We could be angry that they're not paying the taxes they are legally liable for. We could shrug our shoulders and say "So what?" Or we could ask why our tax burden is so high that the only way the government can collect what's due is with the threat of force against people struggling to make it from one month to the next. Further, we could ask what the cost would be of bringing the underground economy into the tax system either by overwhelming force, or by eliminating cash entirely.

All systems need a safety valve, like a water heater or a pressure cooker. If the temperature or the pressure gets too high, the safety valve is released and some of the steam escapes. Yes, some heat is lost, but it assures the continued functioning of the system. The underground cash economy is like a safety valve. When times get tough for a segment of the population, they turn to the cash economy to pay their rent and put food on their table. Without that option, we'd have many more homeless and many more claims for public assistance. All that comes at a high cost. But the underground cash economy is efficient: every dollar earned is spent on something needed or wanted by a family. In the taxed economy, a high percentage of public assistance funds are spent not to help families, but to pay for paper-pushing bureaucrats and administrative employees.

CHAPTER 17

The Patriot Act and Your Cash

SEVERAL YEARS AGO I was helping a relative negotiate a car purchase. As we were filling out the final paperwork and paying for the car, the salesman placed a credit application on the table and asked that certain personal information be filled in. I protested, saying that the car was not being purchased on credit. My relative was going to write a personal check for the entire purchase price of the automobile. The salesman said that it doesn't matter: the government requires that the information be collected in order to be checked against a database of known terrorists. I was taken aback. He explained further that the information also had to be reported to the IRS because the car was being purchased for cash greater than $10,000. I again protested, saying that a personal check is not cash. He insisted it was indeed cash. We filled out the required paperwork and took the car home, but it left us both with a feeling of being suspects of a crime and of having our privacy invaded.

Later, I looked up the rules to confirm I was right. A personal check is not considered cash, either for the IRS reporting or for FinCEN reporting. I concluded that, the auto dealership most likely makes their salespeople collect information on all customers to make sure they don't make a mistake that could cost them thousands of dollars if the government comes calling. The information is in their files, even if they never need it and even if it was not technically required for a particular transaction. The car dealer does not want to place their salespeople in a position of having to make the determination of who and what is reportable. They want them to sell cars.

The PATRIOT Act: Providing Appropriate Tools Required to Intercept and Obstruct Terrorism Act. Who thinks up these acronyms?

Great, but what does the Patriot Act have to do with cash? This book is supposed to be about the war on cash, not the war on "terror." Just as the government believes that they can thwart fraud, drug sales, and tax evasion by tracking cash transactions, so too they believe they can thwart terrorists by doing the same.

The PATRIOT Act expands the Banking Secrecy Act, which authorizes the Treasury to write regulations to make financial institutions keep certain records and to report certain transactions to the IRS. The PATRIOT Act has more stringent requirements regarding verification of customer identity: it expands anti-money laundering efforts to industries not previously covered; expands money laundering regulations to foreign branches of U.S. banks, as well as to foreign institutions operating in the United States; and increases civil and criminal penalties for money laundering.[17.1]

Under the PATRIOT Act, signed into law by President George Bush in 2001 in the wake of the attacks on the World Trade Center and the Pentagon, certain businesses must disclose certain cash transactions to the government. What are these "certain businesses" that are required to make such disclosures? They are referred to as "financial institutions" in the PATRIOT Act but, as you'll see, any business can be shoe-horned into that category. Some of the businesses that are considered financial institutions under Title III of the US PATRIOT Act include casinos, real estate brokers, pawn brokers, travel agencies, jewelers, automobile retailers, and boat retailers.[17.2]

While all businesses are required to report cash transactions in excess of $10,000, under the PATRIOT Act, financial institutions have to go a lot further than that in their surveillance and in fulfilling their responsibility to verify the identity of their customer. A "financial institution" has to check a customer's name against twelve different lists maintained by nine federal agencies to determine if the person has to be reported to the government.[17.3] One list is the Specially Designated Nationals List (SDN).[17.4] This was the reason for my discomfort in having to disclose sensitive personal information during a car purchase — information that had nothing to do with buying a car, but could facilitate identity theft. I wonder how many terrorists or money launderers have been taken off the streets as a result of trying to buy a car?

Like it or not, it appears the PATRIOT Act is here to stay, and it is a powerful tool in the hands of the anti-cash forces.

CHAPTER 18

The Fourth Industrial Revolution Depends on a Cashless Society

FIRST INDUSTRIAL REVOLUTION: Used water and steam to mechanize production.

Second Industrial Revolution: Used electric power to make mass production possible.

Third Industrial Revolution: Used computing technology to automate industry.[18.1]

The "Fourth Industrial Revolution" is a term coined by Klaus Schwab, head of the World Economic Forum. It "describes a world where individuals move between digital domains and offline reality with the use of connected technology to enable and manage their lives."[18.2]

The Fourth Industrial Revolution is the integration of technologies like artificial intelligence, blockchain, virtual reality, biotech, robotics, fintech and the Internet of Things. Rather than being driven by steam, electricity, or computer automation, the fourth industrial revolution is driven by the massive collection of data — your private data. It's about spotting patterns, predicting your behavior, and ultimately changing your behavior. It requires total surveillance, and that means eliminating anonymous cash transactions.

The big financial institutions look out across the landscape of the world and see too many people using cash. Banks and payment processors do not get a cut of cash transactions. There is a big untapped market out there. That's their incentive to bring more people into the system of credit borrowing and electronic transactions. They call it "financial inclusion."

The big corporations know that if they can identify your buying patterns, your moods, your personal situation, your location, your friends, your interests, they can put an offer in front of you at exactly the right moment to get you to make a purchase that you ordinarily would not make.

Governments know there are many economic transactions taking place every day that escape taxation. They see a huge opportunity to increase tax collections by increasing the number of transactions that take place electronically and are thereby easily identified and taxed. Governments also understand that they can easily profile individuals based on their electronic transactions. This will increase oppression of political dissidents. Unlike with cash, digital money will be politicized by allowing the State to deny access to digital money, violating the civil rights of its citizens.

Fourth Industrial Revolution technologies will make it possible for big banks and lenders, big corporations and governments to collect the personal data they need to accomplish their ends: more debt, more taxes, more consumerism, and more control over the behavior of individuals. Having control of the electronic transaction world means the power structure can either allow or deny access to the system to anyone they choose. The ability to use cash diminishes this power.

You may have heard of the "Internet of Things." This describes a world where many everyday objects are connected to the internet and constantly transmit data to who-knows-where. Right now, probably the only things in your home that are transmitting data to corporations, governments, spies and hackers are your personal computer, your tablet, your smart phone, your television cable box, and perhaps your automobile. Many more things will soon be connected to your home Wi-Fi or cell towers: your refrigerator, stove, air conditioning and heating system, lighting fixtures, washer and dryer, garage door opener, lawn mower and many more things. Other items you purchase may have an RFID chip that the internet-connected devices in your house can read.

While the Internet of Things is an incredible tool for mass collection of private data, it is more invasive than gathering data from electronic transactions and will take longer to implement. The low-hanging fruit is everyday economic transactions. Electronic transactions generate far more data to mine than do cash transactions.

The Fourth Industrial Revolution is intensifying and sustaining the war on cash.

CHAPTER 19

Hope for the
Future of Cash

ALTHOUGH POWERFUL INTERESTS ARE aligned against cash, there is effective pushback and resistance on some fronts.

The European Central Bank maintains that it supports the right of consumers to continue to use cash if they choose.

In the United States, Massachusetts has required retail establishments to accept cash since 1978. However, this law has its critics, and it remains to be seen how long it will stay in effect.[19.1]

Philadelphia passed a law in 2019 making it, according to NPR's *All Things Considered*, "the first big city in the country to ban cash-free stores."[19.2]

New York City passed a law that requires all businesses that sell merchandise to accept cash or face a penalty. It started when a city councilman was inconvenienced at a coffee shop when he realized the only form of payment he had on him was cash, and the shop did not accept cash. He promptly introduced a bill to prohibit businesses like that from refusing cash, and it passed, largely on the concern that it marginalized the unbanked.[19.3]

San Francisco, California, and New Jersey also passed laws in 2019 banning cashless businesses. Again, the primary reason is that it's discriminatory and marginalizes the poor.

Such bans are put in place, not because the requirement to use electronic payment cards is "inclusive," but precisely because it is not inclusive of people who do not have bank accounts and debit cards (the "unbanked") and who may not have access to credit.

G4S, a global security company, published a report in 2018 stating that cash is still "in high demand across all continents." It reports that in North America, over 50% of transactions under $25, and 60% of transactions under $10 occurred with cash.

The Global Cash Report quotes a GS4 Chief Executive, Jesus Rosano: "People trust cash; it's free to use and readily available for consumers, it's confidential, it can't be hacked, and it doesn't run out of battery power — these unique qualities continue to hold significant value to people living on all continents."[19.4]

Earlier we learned that some banks in Sweden are refusing to provide their customers with access to cash or charging exorbitant fees for handling cash deposits and withdrawals. CashEssentials. org reports that in November 2019 the European Central Bank published a legal opinion (non-binding) "on the legislative proposal put forward by the Swedish government on 26 September 2019 requiring that large credit institutions provide cash services to the public. The purpose of the law is to ensure an adequate level of access to cash throughout Sweden in a context of ATM closure and branches which no longer enable cash deposits or withdrawals."[19.5] So far there's no word on whether there will be a limitation on fees charged by banks to continue to offer access to cash. The proposed law will only apply to the six largest banks. Riksbank also supports the initiative, but believes it should apply to all banks.

The published opinion by the ECB observes that certain groups of people may have limited access to digital payment technology.

Cash is the only method of payment available to them. It specifically mentions "the elderly, immigrants, the disabled, socially vulnerable citizens and others . . ." It also recognizes that a lack of access to cash could have ". . . a detrimental effect on the security, preparedness and efficiency of the payment market in the event of a major disruption in the payment system" and that cash needs to remain "a functional alternative to electronic payments."[19.6]

On the civil asset forfeiture and structuring front, there has been a continuous effort by legislators to enact laws that limit the ability of governments to seize cash without serious evidence that it was being used in criminal activity. Some successes have been realized, but there's still a long way to go.

Who will win the war on cash? I'm not sure there will be a clear winner. Most likely there will be some type of compromise. Unless serious opposition is rallied to the cause, ordinary people will probably be left only with the ability to make small purchases with cash; all other financial transactions will have to be electronic. I can see the eventual elimination of all denominations of US currency above the twenty-dollar bill. But the battle isn't over yet. The biggest success so far achieved by the anti-cash cabal is their successful campaign to brainwash people into believing that only criminals and tax evaders conduct their affairs in cash, and that it is consumers who are demanding digital payment systems. These myths have to be effectively countered.

CHAPTER 20

What Can You Do?

RESISTANCE OFTEN SEEMS FUTILE. Start talking about liberty, privacy, the constitution, the war on cash, the militarization of law enforcement, and people look at you like you're one of those to-be-avoided-at-all-costs "right-wing nut jobs" still "clinging to their guns and religion."

Why don't people care more about the problem of the seizure of cash from innocent people by law enforcement? Why are they so uncomfortable when the topic is broached? I got some insight into this from the Tom Woods Show podcast episode #348. Woods is a liberty-minded scholar, historian, author and prolific podcaster. He interviewed Warren Redlich of FairDUI .org who is the author of the book *Fair DUI: Stay Safe and Sane in a World Gone MADD*, and offers his opinion (at 24:00 in the podcast) on the observation that most people are not sympathetic to the problem of innocent people being dragged through the legal system.[20.1] Redlich asserts that people don't realize the costs innocent people have to pay. They may have a mug shot published on the internet and in the local newspaper. They have legal fees and court and administrative costs and a record of their arrest in a national database.

Of course Redlich is talking about it in the context of DUI stops and sobriety tests, but the same concepts apply to structuring charges and civil asset forfeiture. Just as Mothers Against Drunk Drivers benefits when innocent people are arrested for suspicion of DUI because it furthers their agenda of scaring people away from consuming even the smallest amount of alcohol before driving, so politicians, activists, banks, law enforcement, the IRS and government agencies benefit when cash is stolen from innocent people through civil asset forfeiture: it makes people afraid to use cash for fear of arousing suspicion and being reported to the government.

What can one person do to resist an ever-growing government's encroachment on liberty? The first step is simply to be aware of what's happening and how it's happening. The next step is to talk about it with your friends and family. Make sure they see what's happening and how it will affect them.

Some people will not be interested. Some will call you a conspiracy nut. Others will take the time to look up from their smartphone long enough to let you know they think that getting rid of cash is a very good idea.

Don't waste your time trying to convince anyone. Look for people who will listen and who agree that there's a war on cash and that getting rid of cash is a bad idea. Discuss the problem with them and share ideas on how to resist. The internet is a good place to connect with people who share your concern, and most of those people will happily share their ideas about how to fight back.

One person can't solve all the problems, but he can make an attempt to dodge, frustrate, or overcome the problems that most affect his life. There is no easy, one-size-fits-all remedy. You will have to find your own way. In the following chapters, I'll put forth some possibilities that might be appealing to some. They are not my own original ideas. Perhaps they're no one's original ideas. But they are ideas. Make them yours if you wish.

CHAPTER 21

Unbanking

THE TERM "UNBANKED" HAS generally been applied to people who do not keep their money in a bank. Not long ago, people who handled their financial affairs without banks began to use the term in an empowering way, as in "We don't need no stinkin' banks." Quite a few of them are not poor or broke, though many became unbanked because they went through financial difficulties and felt abused by their financial institution. Many of the unbanked, of course, are in that situation because they either do not have enough cash to maintain a bank balance, or they have poor money management skills.

A surprising number of people are choosing to keep their money outside of banks — about 40 million Americans don't have bank accounts.[21.1] If you add the underbanked — people who use both banks and bank alternatives — the number may be as high as 70 million. Usually they unbank because of high account-related fees, high bounced-check fees, and the general feeling that banks are evil. During the Occupy Wall Street movement, we saw a wave of humanity (who could probably afford bank fees) abandoning banks and either joining the great unbanked or moving their money to credit unions, which in many cases are not much better than banks, and sometimes a good deal worse.

Abandoning banks completely means entering the world of prepaid debit cards, pay day lenders, check cashing services and rent-to-own merchants. The fees associated with those transaction-based services can easily approach ten percent of the amount of the transactions. That means for a person earning $25,000 per year, non-bank transaction processing fees could exceed $2,000. That's probably a high estimate, and no doubt a savvy user of bank alternatives could do better, but the fact remains that alternative financial transaction services can be prohibitively expensive.

The bottom line: avoiding banks is expensive and inconvenient. For those who have no choice, the price and the hassle have to be borne. For the rest, a bank-free life is only for the most dedicated and determined, and is most likely to be successful when combined with other strategies to reduce your dependence on the dollar as suggested by Daisy Luther, author and owner of The Organic Prepper website. Here are some of Daisy's suggestions from a section of one of her blog posts under the sub-heading Ditch the Dollar.[21,2]

- Engage in the barter system: trade goods and services with like-minded people.

- Keep precious metals like gold and silver in a fireproof safe for your "savings account."

- Immediately convert fiat currency into tangible goods: food, ammo, home defense items, tools, etc.

- Work towards self-sufficiency — if you buy less, you can earn less: grow your food, repair your own home or vehicle, do things manually instead of using expensive equipment, lessen your dependency on the grid.

- Simplify — this goes hand-in-hand with self-sufficiency: find your entertainment from library books and online resources, skip eating out, take a walk instead of joining a gym. The less you feel you need, the less money you will have to earn.

Probably the most workable strategy for the average person who wants to distance themselves from banks is to use a bank account as a clearing account. Deposit just enough to cover your bills and maintain the required minimum balance to avoid a service charge. Take any excess out as cash. But remember, regular withdrawals that look like you might be trying to avoid the dreaded Currency Transaction Report could get you in trouble. Withdrawing one or two thousand dollars cash from your account once or twice each month should not be a problem. (That's not intended to be legal advice). Obviously, this won't work with retirement accounts and IRAs, although if you don't trust banks, I'm not sure why you'd have an IRA or retirement account other than through an employer-sponsored plan that matches employee contributions.

CHAPTER 22

Safely Hiding Cash

IF YOU DECIDE NOT to place all your cash in the bank, you'll need to conceal it in a safe place.

Hiding cash is nothing new. Many people before the mid-1900's did not trust banks, so they kept what money they had squirreled away in some pretty creative places. This is the beauty of cash — you don't have to keep it in a financial institution.

CNBC reports an American Express survey shows about 29% of people admit to keeping a stash of cash and coin outside the bank.[22.1] The most common hiding places are in the freezer or in a sock drawer. Burglars must have been thrilled to read that report.

There are a number of books and web articles with ideas for hiding cash around the home. For the most part, these resources don't contain new or groundbreaking information. Interviews with burglars over the years reveal that they know about all the hiding places and will tear your house apart looking for cash.

Lots of training and information-sharing take place in prisons. In my opinion, the most effective hiding place for cash is buried securely somewhere on your property, preferably in multiple locations among decoy caches. A quality home safe is also an attractive alternative, but it must be securely attached to the foundation. If you purchase a safe, be sure to understand what exactly it protects against. Is it fire resistant? Flood resistant? Or just burglar resistant? A good safe is expensive. It's probably not a good idea to spend $1,000 on a safe to store only $2,500 worth of cash and valuables.

Hiding cash in books, papers, cans, in walls, in the freezer, etc. are all places known to smart burglars. Of course, not all burglars are smart. Multiple well-thought-out hiding places around the house may in many cases be effective against the average meth addict looking for quick cash in the master bedroom dresser.

Possession of anything valuable — cash, art, jewelry, electronics, collectibles, firearms, tools — is a risk. A segment of the population seems to have as their life purpose the transferring of your stuff to them. Not all of them are elected officials. Your valuables are at risk whether they are in a bank or in your freezer. Different types of risk to be sure, but risk just the same. People who lost their life savings to Bernard Madoff or Enron are no less devastated than those whose savings were pilfered from the freezer by a burglar.

Since cash cannot be traced, it is particularly risky to attempt to hide it.

The modern world has devised a way to deal with risk. It's called insurance. Insurance won't prevent your cash from being stolen, but it will transfer the risk of loss to the insurance company. Banks use the FDIC to insure your money up to $250,000 (though that won't help if all or most of the major banks fail at the same time). Some homeowner's or renter's insurance policies may offer an insurance policy rider against cash theft. Most likely there are limits, but be sure to ask your insurance company.

There are no perfect, risk-free solutions.

An important consideration when hiding significant amounts of cash is what will happen if you should later decide to put it in the bank, or if you need to make a large purchase (more than $10,000). Remember that depositing more than $10,000 cash into a bank will generate a Currency Transaction Report and could result in a visit from law enforcement or the IRS. Making a purchase for more than $10,000 could also result in a report being sent to the IRS or law enforcement.

You could find yourself in the position of having to prove that the cash you've hidden was obtained legally or that you did in fact earn the money and paid taxes on it. The best way I can think of to do this is to first be sure the money was deposited in your bank account. If it was taxable income, it should also be traceable to your tax return. When you withdraw the money to put in your safe (or wherever), write a check to yourself and keep a copy. Or make a photocopy of any withdrawal receipt. Next, record the serial numbers of each bill. It's not a perfect solution, but it may increase your chances of keeping your money from being seized. Understand that it is illegal to photocopy or photograph paper currency in the United States.

CHAPTER 23

Transporting Cash

THIS REALLY IS THE tip of the spear. Cash is at its most vulnerable while it is being moved from place to place, whether on your person, in your car, or in a package or envelope in possession of a common carrier. Naturally, this is where the government focuses much of its efforts. The government wants you to be afraid to carry, transport, or spend cash.

As you may recall from this book's sections on civil asset forfeiture, most seizures of cash occurred because the individuals were intimidated by the presence of the law enforcement officers and consented to being searched, assuming that they had nothing illegal to hide. In many cases, a polite refusal to be searched could have ended the matter. Of course, if you're riding a bus or train or plane, you probably consent to a search when you buy the ticket — read the fine print. This is not the case when you're in your own home or car or when you're walking down the street.

Being polite to a law enforcement officer is the best approach in all circumstances. Offer respect. If you don't respect law enforcement, at least pretend that you do. "All the world's a stage," and all that. You can do it.

Most legal experts say you should produce your I.D. or driver's license, registration and car insurance proof when appropriate, but not answer questions or consent to any searches. Lawyers often disagree on some of the fine points. For instance, in Arrest-Proof Yourself, attorney and former law enforcement officer Dale C. Carson advises against consenting to searches.[23.1] However, he allows if you're absolutely sure your car is "clean," the quickest way to get it over with may be to let the cop search. But remember, Carson used to be a cop.

Law enforcement officers are trained to ask a series of questions to gather evidence against you. Any inconsistencies in your answers or any signs of nervousness or fear can create "reasonable suspicion." Like they say, anything you say can and will be used against you in a court of law. It will not be used for your benefit, only against you. Many of the nation's top defense attorneys say that you should never talk to the police.[23.2]

If you value your cash, carrying it in an envelope laying on your front seat or stashed under your seat is not a great idea. Having it stuffed in a backpack or in a bag in the trunk is not a great idea either. The best idea is not to carry large amounts of cash. If you do, be a little more careful about where you put it. Consider using a well-made money belt. Consider not keeping it all together in one location. Ultimately there's no foolproof way to conceal a large amount of cash from a determined law enforcement officer. They'll tear your car apart panel by panel if they suspect you're hiding something.

Ultimately, the best tactic is to not be stopped by the police. If the police don't see you, they won't stop you. Be invisible to law enforcement. Blend in. Some call it "the gray man" approach. Attorney and former police officer Dale Carson gets more specific about the driver profile that is a police magnet and is just begging to be searched. You're an attractive target for law enforcement if you're driving too fast, too slow, or erratically; if your car has an expired tag, its lights are not working properly, has rust, dents, and bad tires, a messy interior or cracked glass, dark-tinted windows; three or four males occupy it, look like thugs, use foul language, are playing loud music or are arguing, have an open container, are not wearing seatbelts, smell of alcohol or dope, have clothing with offensive language or symbols common to gangs; "hate-literature" is present in the vehicle; occupants are reaching around in the vehicle and their hands cannot be seen; the driver has a suspended license or no insurance.[23.3]

You get the idea. Don't look like someone that might be carrying illegal things, and you can reduce your chances of being stopped and searched.

But what if you need to move $50,000 in cash from, say, Miami, Florida to Flagstaff, Arizona? Perhaps you're moving cross country and need to transport cash from your home safe. I'm assuming that your cash was legally earned and you paid taxes on it. In other words, you're doing nothing wrong — you just prefer not to have your cash in a financial institution for privacy reasons.

Why not let the US Postal Service move the money for you? Privacy expert JJ Luna says you can mail five $100 bills in a business size #10 envelope anywhere in the United States (he advises against cross-border mailing of cash).[23.4] Luna suggests mailing the envelopes from various locations over a period of several days or weeks using normal first-class mail. It would probably be a good idea to mail to multiple destinations in your new location if possible. It's not a perfect and risk-free solution, but it virtually eliminates the possibility of seizure by an over-zealous law enforcement officer, and it appears to be legal as of this writing.

Purchasing large amounts of traveler's checks or money orders will trigger a Currency Transaction Report or possibly a Suspicious Activity Report. I see no reason why these paper financial instruments could not be seized just like cash.

CHAPTER 24

Legislation. Organization. Infiltration. Disobedience. Tactics.

OTHER THAN ATTEMPTING TO guard your personal privacy and not to break laws that you're aware of, there isn't a lot you as an individual can do to protect yourself against the war on cash. Fighting back against such a powerful, entrenched and virtually lawless system is difficult. Civil disobedience is problematic, because about half of the people in the United States and an even greater percentage in other countries think it's okay for the government to confiscate your cash if you look suspicious, and would be perfectly happy if cash were abolished. They think that if you're using cash and trying to maintain your privacy that you must be a criminal or a tax dodge. They believe that government abuses of power are few and unusual (until it happens to them or their favorite protected group) and that a few abuses here and there need to be tolerated in order to have a compliant society.

For civil disobedience to work, you have to have the general public on your side, which means juries will be on your side. Like it or not, the US is an increasingly collectivist and redistributionist country, and the Constitution has been overridden by regulations written and enforced by unelected bureaucrats and a judiciary afraid to hew to the Constitution for fear of being deemed irrelevant by a mostly statist and collectivist population. On top of that, we have a power-drunk executive branch and legislative bodies whose main focus is fundraising for their next election cycle.

Charles Murray, in his fine book By the People: Rebuilding Liberty Without Permission, gives an example of civil disobedience that is entirely effective.[24.1] On any highway on any day, almost every driver exceeds the posted speed limit. There's no way law enforcement can ticket all of them, or even most of them. So they choose to enforce the speed limit against only those drivers who are driving so fast (or so slow) that they endanger the flow of traffic, or against drivers that fit the profile of someone who may be carrying illegal items. In this case, the enforcement mechanism is overwhelmed by wide-spread and popular acts of disobedience and is forced to effect a "no harm, no foul" enforcement policy. Even the judges and law-makers break the speed limit on the way to and from work every day. Unfortunately, public sympathies are currently not as strong toward privacy and the use of cash as they are toward fast driving.

As I've shown, the attacks on the use of cash are coming from government, financial services firms, academics, and nonprofits. The only non-violent way to stop them is to turn their own methods against them. Exert influence on your legislators. Let them know of your concerns. Support legislation introduced to combat civil asset forfeiture. Recruit scholars with competing theories to publish papers and speak at conferences in support of the existence of cash. Buy their books and subscribe to and share their social media channels.

Support nonprofits that formulate and encourage cash-friendly and privacy-friendly policies. Use social media to connect with like-minded people and spread the word. Consider forming your own local group and link up with regional partners. The people who are trying to abolish cash have been doing this for years. They have a head start.

Are you thinking of a career in academia? This is a great way to infiltrate the machine that is helping to lend justification to negative interest rates and the abolishment of cash. Get inside the system. Publish papers and lecture on the folly of a cash-free society.

Do you think voting is a waste of time? Fine. No problem. Don't vote. But don't let that stop you from participating in the movement to keep cash around for yourself and for future generations.

Finally, let's talk about some boots-on-the-ground tactics. The first and most important tactic is tough. You're probably not going to like it at all, but it is perhaps the single most important thing you can do to throw a monkey-wrench into the gears of globalism and the war on cash. Ready?

Get rid of your smart phone.

Cancel your plan, delete your files, reset the phone, remove the SIM card and sell your phone on eBay.

Your smart phone is a spy device. That is the purpose of your phone — to gather data about your behaviors and transmit it to corporations to be sold, and to the government in case they ever need to investigate you. Your cell phone transmits your exact location to Google or Apple twenty four hours a day, seven days a week. In the bathroom? In the kitchenware section of Walmart? Driving your car? At the gun store? Google knows. It's recorded forever. Every app on your phone transmits data back to the programmers who created the app. Every app on your phone listens to what you're saying. Every app has access to your photos, your microphone, and your text messages. Every time you make a purchase, click on an ad, view an ad, the information is used to build a profile about you that can be sold to corporations or which can be turned over to the government, including the FBI, TSA, Homeland Security, ATF, and any other letter combination created by Uncle Sam. As long as you're a walking transmitter, you have no privacy whether you use cash or electronic transactions. Your phone is like an ankle bracelet for a criminal sentenced to home arrest.

If you can't bring yourself to get rid of your smart phone, there are actions you can take to minimize the amount of spying it can do. Setting it to "airplane mode" is not an effective action. It is still gathering data even though it is not transmitting. Once you take it off airplane mode it releases a torrent of data back to the mother ship.

Delete apps like Facebook and Instagram. Get rid of every app you don't need. They gather and transmit data that will be sold and cross-matched in countless databases. Get a dumb phone. You know, one of those flip phones that only makes and receives calls and doesn't access the internet. Leave your smart phone at the office or at home. When you leave, take only your dumb phone with you to make and receive calls. If you must have your smart phone with you "just in case," buy an RFID signal blocking pouch for it. Get a high-quality bag, not one of those $10 bags sold on Amazon. I get mine from a company called "Mission Darkness." You can find them on the web. They specialize in selling such things to law enforcement. Whenever you're out and about, put your phone in the bag. As long as it is properly sealed in the bag it can neither transmit nor receive data from the internet. It cannot record your location or determine your speed or direction. It cannot make or receive calls or text messages. I presume it can hear your voice though.

To see how easily people can be controlled by their smart phone, you need only look at what's going on in China. Alibaba — China's Amazon — has created an app for use by the Chinese government that tracks people's movements to see if they've been in close contact with someone infected with the coronavirus. Users are assigned a color code based on their exposure profile. To enter buildings or visit certain areas of over 200 cities, users must scan a QR code to find out whether they are allowed to proceed.[24.2] Some people are confined to their homes based on their color code, unable even to go and buy food or go to work. Of course this isn't the first time China has used smartphone apps and facial recognition to monitor and control their citizens.

If you're thinking that can't happen in the United States or Canada, you probably haven't heard about the "Locate X" software sold by Babel Street. US law enforcement agencies have millions of dollars worth of contracts with Babel Street to use this software that tracks the movement of people's cell phones. This software allows a user to specify a specific location or area. It then identifies all mobile devices that have been within that area as well as where else those devices have traveled, going back months.[24.3]

Locate X can also be used to collect data anonymously for sale to data brokers. There is no question that such a tool can be a great benefit to law enforcement. But the potential for abuse is high. Presently this ability to monitor and restrict the movements of people is largely dependent on smartphones. As facial recognition software becomes more widely adopted, any hope of anonymity vanishes. The ability to use cash at that point may become crucial to survival for anyone outside the politically correct bubble.

Do not install devices in your home like the Amazon Echo or Alexa. That's just handing your innermost secrets and private moments to the corporate machine.

Cash. Use it or lose it. Pay for your groceries with cash. Buy gasoline with cash. Make your department store and discount store purchases in person with cash and avoid using their discount cards whenever possible. Those cards are just another way to gather data on your behavior and preferences so they can sell it. But of course, avoid carrying too much cash at once.

Teach your children the advantages of liquidity and the anonymity of cash.

Recognize that many battles will be fought in the war on cash. This isn't going to be settled overnight. It will be an uphill struggle, especially as the younger generation matures into positions of power. Many of the younger generation seem to be willing to give up nearly everything for convenience and entertainment. So, think about how you will avoid having your wealth confiscated by negative interest rates, inflation, and taxation. Consider turning your cash into hard assets that will maintain their value. Quality tools, household supplies, clothing items, etc. What will be in short supply if the dollar collapses suddenly? What items will you certainly need and use in the future that you can purchase and store safely today?

Many people stack silver, gold, firearms, and ammo. Those items will always have value, but will they always be legal to possess? That's something we each have to take into account when determining how much of each to invest in.

What will a simple 2002 Toyota Camry in good running condition be worth in another ten years when every car that comes off an assembly line is chocked full of sensors, transmitters and microphones that send gigabytes of private data about you to mega-corporations and to a government that is increasingly hostile to anyone with a sense of independence and liberty.

What success has been achieved by any of the above methods? It is not unreasonable to take the position that the battle is already lost and that any successes in the battle against financial tyranny are too little, too late to be of lasting impact. But as we have seen, media exposure, lawsuits by nonprofit legal assistance organizations, and individual contacts with legislators have resulted in the Department of Justice and the IRS's backing down to some extent on cash seizures related to alleged structuring activities and resulted in the federal government's backing off slightly on seizures of cash from citizens who are "carrying too much cash" but not otherwise committing a crime. This can be counted as a success, and it didn't happen by citizens rolling over and playing dead.

Despite the constant pressure from governments and financial institutions and the collectivist intellectual class that supports and justifies their attempts to move away from cash, considerable strength is being used to counteract those freedom and privacy reducing forces.

If you're a liberty-minded person and you find yourself from time to time engaged, in person or through social media, in debates with people who believe your personal liberty ought in all cases subordinate to the collective, to the needs of "society," you will often feel overwhelmed. Overwhelmed by the prepared talking points and coordinated tactics, the well-rehearsed and facile narratives, the re-framing of the debate, the re-defining of terms that now seem to mean something other than what they once did, the charging of collective guilt, the virtue-signaling, and the fervor with which those talking points and tactics are applied. You will find yourself debating those who know more about historical trivia than you do; with those who know more about economic theory and monetary policy; with those whose rhetorical sleight-of-hand may cow you into silence, into questioning your values and philosophy.

Fear not.

When confronted with such uncomfortable situations, do not allow yourself to be pulled into technical debates. Understand that you're not responsible for "converting" by argumentation those with strongly held opposing viewpoints.

It is equally important to understand the bounds of liberty. Individual liberty is always constrained to those actions that do not reduce another person's liberty, now or in the future.

The elimination of or restriction of cash greatly reduces individual liberty. It is the face of evil.

Wealth and Money

NOTE: FOLLOWING IS A SIMPLIFIED explanation of the relationship between wealth and money, why we have money, and what money really is. These concepts are the key to understanding money. If you do not understand this chapter, you will never understand money or wealth. I have made it simple enough so that anyone with an eighth grade reading ability should be able to understand it. I've placed it in the appendix to this book because is not central to my thesis and will not be needed by all readers, many of whom already understand the concepts. It is written for those readers who are convinced that money is evil and that life without money would be better. That is equivalent to thinking, after a plane crash that gravity is evil and life would be better without it.

You don't need a PhD in economics to understand money. You just need to get the basics down, and the basics are pretty simple.

Most of us think of wealth by picturing someone standing next to their Rolls Royce parked in front of their 50 room mansion with house servants. But that's not a helpful understanding. It's an extreme. Here's a better way to understand wealth: Imagine yourself on a tropical island with a few other people. There is a coral reef full of fish, lots of lush coconut palms, and various trees and seabirds. You have nothing else. No knife, no fish hooks. No boat. Nothing. You do have some beautiful natural resources and you could count that as wealth, but it really isn't wealth until you do something with it. You cannot eat the fish until you catch them. You cannot eat or drink the coconuts until you harvest them and somehow crack them open to get to the edible part. If you get sick or injured, there is no medicine or medical supplies.

Being industrious people, you and your island neighbors get right to work and find some sharp shells to use as cutting tools. You gather some palm fibers to make fishing nets and rope. You build a shelter from the beautiful palm fronds. You use your net to catch lots of fish, which you dry in the hot tropical sun. From the coconuts you produce oil to protect your skin from the harsh sun and constant sea wind. By having an excess food supply of dried fish and coconuts stored, you have some free time to explore the inner parts of the island to look for edible fruits and plants, to gather bird eggs, and to harvest wood to make more tools. Now you have created wealth!

Wealth is something you have harvested or built that sustains life. It feeds you, it quenches your thirst, it heals you, it makes you more comfortable, it frees up your time to create more wealth. It frees up your time to think and to create and to share. Wealth exists even without money. Now go back to the beginning of this scenario before anyone made a fishing net or harvested a coconut or did any physical work. Suppose everyone just sat around getting hungry and sunburned but didn't try to do anything about it. Imagine that just when it looked like they would all starve, a big package washed up onto the beach. Everyone rushed over and tore open the package. Inside was one million dollars in fresh, clean, dry currency.

They're now rich beyond their wildest dreams, right? Not exactly, since there is nothing on the island to buy. No one has anything to sell. The money is useless except perhaps to use as toilet paper or kindling for a fire. So there you have it. Money is not wealth. This may seem obvious to you, but I can assure you it is not obvious to most people, even to certain famous economists who shall remain unnamed. We'll be coming back to this idea in a more contemporary and relevant setting, so don't forget. Money is not wealth.

For now, let's go back to our beautiful tropical island where our survivors have created a nice little island paradise with plenty of surplus food and drink. One of the islanders has found some yummy edible berries and has saved the seeds and planted a nice patch of berry plants. He has put a lot of work into his little berry garden even though everyone else said he was wasting his time. It took three years and a lot of watering and weeding and careful tending to have a nice harvest. As soon as he brings his harvest back to the "village" everyone wants some berries. Since there is no money on the island, they use the barter system, which means they trade amongst themselves.

The best fishermen offer him some fresh fish in exchange for berries and he makes the trade. The tool maker offers him a new shell knife in exchange for some berries. Unfortunately our berry gardener already has enough shell knives and is not willing to trade his berries for another knife. This, unfortunately is the limitation of the barter system. It gets complicated very quickly if you don't have what the other person wants or needs. The problem is that one person wants to trade wealth that he has created for wealth that another person has created, but what one has to offer is not needed by the other. What is needed is some system to make that exchange of wealth happen even when the berry gardener does not want or need a shell knife. How can we facilitate a transaction so the shell knife maker can get some berries to eat?

At this point some argumentative types will observe that in such a small "economy" the villagers would probably divide up the berries equally. This is probably true, but does not represent what happens in a larger economy. I'm trying to simplify what happens in a larger economy, so you'll just have to accept the limitations in my example.

What the villagers need is something that they can trade which represents the wealth they have created. That's the purpose of money. Money represents wealth that has been created but not yet consumed. In our village, some type of "money" is adopted and is assigned to producers in accordance with how much wealth they have produced and according to the agreed rate of exchange (one coconut shell full of berries is equal to two tuna fish or whatever). Now the shell knife maker can buy some berries with his money, and he can sell his shell knives to someone who needs them in exchange for money.

Now we have a system of exchange money in place to facilitate the buying and selling of goods and services. As we have already seen, the money itself is of no value without the goods and services it represents. So, for example, if whoever is in charge of money decides to arbitrarily distribute a large amount of new money among the villagers even though no new berries were grown, no new fish were caught, and no new shell knives were made, you can see that the new money has no value whatsoever since it represents nothing. No new wealth has been produced. The villagers are no better off as a result of receiving the new money.

The result of distributing new and worthless money is that the purchasing power of each dollar already in existence is reduced by the amount of new worthless money that was distributed to the villagers. So then, what is the definition of money we've developed? Here is the definition: Money is a fungible representation of wealth created but not consumed. Or to use the words of another thinker, Ann Barnhardt: it is a "fungible proxy." Fungible just means that every dollar is just like every other dollar. A dollar bill in my pocket is exactly the same and is indistinguishable from a dollar bill in your pocket. Fungible. Rice grains are fungible. "Proxy" just means "representative." A dollar is a representative of or a proxy for a shell knife that was created by physical labor, just like a ticket to the Super Bowl is a proxy for the money you paid in exchange for the right to occupy a seat in the stadium for the duration of the game.

The existence of money does not devalue the barter (trade) experience. There is nothing wrong with bartering whenever possible. I highly recommend it. Barter systems and time banks are awesome. But barter isn't enough to have a vibrant economy. Money is necessary.

A deeper look into what money is must inevitably lead us to the realization that money represents a portion of our life. If someone spends four hours installing bathroom plumbing in a house and earns $600 for doing that work, the $600 represents four hours of that person's life and effort. It is a fungible proxy for the plumber's time and efforts. If someone robs the plumber and steals the $600, it is the same as stealing four hours of the plumber's life. The robber took four hours of the plumber's life. This is a type of limited slavery. The robber forced the plumber to work for him for four hours without pay, against his will. Slavery. Not the traditional form, but slavery nonetheless. When someone takes your money without your permission — by use of coercion or force — they are taking a part of your life that you can never get back.

So far we've been talking about marketable goods and services. But not everything has a market value. Some readers by now have probably become somewhat disgusted that I've placed such importance on money — that I've made it seem like a thing has no value except that which can be measured in dollars. It is entirely true that there are many valuable things in the world that cannot be bought and sold on any market. What is the price of the love of a devoted mother and father? What is the price of a dear friend? What is the price of a kind act from a Good Samaritan? The love and nurturing of a devoted father is priceless, yes, but it cannot be traded for groceries, or for a car, or for heart surgery. Those items require the ability to exchange goods and services which have a market exchange value. They require money. The existence of and need for marketable products does not in any way detract from or devalue or de-emphasize the importance and values of non-marketable aspects of life. Culture sometimes devalues those things, but the existence of a market does not.

NOTES

Preface

1. Fox, Karla Harbin. Another Step Toward the Cashless Society? The 1978 Federal Electronic Fund Transfer Act. American Business Law Journal, Vol 18, Issue 2, June 1980.

Chapter 1

1.1 Tide Laundry detergent as money. http://nymag.com/news/features/tide-detergent-drugs-2013-1/

1.2 Honeybuns as currency. https://www.prisonlegalnews.org/news/2011/jul/15/the-incredible-honey-bun-behind-bars/

1.3 Federal Reserve website: https://www.federalreserve.gov/faqs.htm

1.4 Two-thirds of US currency held outside the US. http://www.ny.frb.org/aboutthefed/fedpoint/fed49.html

1.5 I've seen estimates as high as $4,000 cash per person, but am not privy to the calculations involved in those estimates. Obviously these estimates are averages and do not reveal the actual distribution of circulating cash.

Chapter 2

2.1 Nordic countries lead the way to cashless society: http://www.reuters.com/article/2015/01/09/us-nordic-cashless-idUSKBN0KI1AA20150109

2.2 Riksbank survey report: https://www.riksbank.se/globalassets/media/statistik/betalningsstatistik/2018/payments-patterns-in-sweden-2018.pdf

2.3 Sweden cashless by 2023: https://knowledge.wharton.upenn.edu/article/going-cashless-can-learn-swedens-experience/

2.4 Swedish banks not accepting cash deposits:DW Documentary "A World Without Money: How Cash is Becoming a Thing of the Past" https://youtu.be/GbECT1J9bXg 7:38 minutes into 42:25 video.

2.5 World's most cashless countries: http://www.cnbc.com/id/102187335

2.6 Sweden cash: https://www.cnbc.com/2018/05/03/sweden-cashless-future-sounds-alarm-bells-for-the-central-bank.html

2.7 France tightens controls on cash: http://mobile.reuters.com/article/idUSKBN0ME14720150318?irpc=932

2.8 European cash limitations: https://www.europe-consommateurs.eu/en/consumer-topics/financial-services-insurance/banking/means-of-payment/cash-payment-limitations/

2.9 European cash limitations: https://www.bragmybag.com/cash-transaction-limits/

2.10 France to fight terrorism: http://mobile.reuters.com/article/idUSKBN0ME14720150318?irpc=932

2.11 France, cash, and terrorism: https://
www.zerohedge.com/news/2015-03-31/
france-moves-direction-banning-cash

2.12 Joseph Salerno Mises Institute lecture:
The War on Cash. https://youtu.be/
x2JPLADXkjU?list=PLALopHfWkFlFTj__lkebZfUw5s
-CWVuIt

2.13 Louisiana Act No. 389: https://legiscan.com/LA/text/
HB195/id/343620

2.14 Cantrell CPA web site: https://cantrellcpa.typepad.com/

2.15 Ackel, Esq. article: Cash Transactions Banned by
Louisiana: Government Takes Private Property Without
Due Process. http://www.sott.net/article/236218-Cash
-Transactions-Banned-by-Louisiana-Government-Takes
-Private-Property-Without-Due-Process

2.16 Chase Bank joins the war on cash: https://mises.org/
blog/chase-joins-war-cash

2.17 Chase safe deposit box agreement: https://www.chase.
com/content/dam/chase-ux/documents/personal/
branch-disclosures/safe-deposit-box-lease-agreement.pdf

2.18 Mises Institute Facebook post by Joe Salerno.
https://www.facebook.com/mises.institute/
posts/10152918534493935

2.19 Kiplinger warning: https://www.kiplinger.com/
slideshow/saving/T005-S001-things-you-ll-regret
-keeping-in-a-safe-deposit-box/index.html

2.20 Visa Cashless Challenge https://usa.visa.com/about-visa/
newsroom/press-releases.releaseId.10926.html

2.21 $10,000 to opt in https://money.cnn.com/2017/07/14/
news/companies/visa-no-cash-restaurant-initiative/
index.html

2.22 Greece forces electronic spending: https://news.
theceomagazine.com/law/greece-kyriakos-mitsotakis/

2.23 Brett Scott opinion in The Guardian: https://www.
theguardian.com/commentisfree/2018/jul/19/
cashless-society-con-big-finance-banks-closing-atms

Chapter 3

3.1 Federal Reserve on removal of large bills: http://www.
federalreserve.gov/faqs/currency_12600.htm and
http://www.treasury.gov/resource-center/faqs/Currency/
Pages/denominations.aspx

3.2 The following U.S. Embassy reference to why large
bills were removed from circulation is no longer
available: http://iipdigital.usembassy.gov/st/english/
article/2013/04/20130410145531.html

However, the exact language now appears on
the following website: https://geneva.usmission.
gov/2013/04/11/u-s-dollars-designed-to-outsmart
-counterfeiters/

3.3 A Google internet search in March 2020 for the search
phrase "Nixon Executive Order on July 14, 1969 removing
all large bills from circulation" (without quotation marks)
returns over one million results.

3.4 Presidential Executive Orders. http://www.presidency
.ucsb.edu/executive_orders.php?year=1969&Submit=
DISPLAY

3.5 Nixon's Special Message to the Congress on Control of
Narcotics and Dangerous Drugs. https://www.presidency
.ucsb.edu/documents/special-message-the-congress
-control-narcotics-and-dangerous-drugs

3.6 Text of joint Treasury / Federal Reserve press release on
July 14, 1969: http://www.panix.com/~clay/
currency/14-Jul-1969.html

Chapter 4

4.1 Remarks by Patrick Heningsen of Global Research. http://
www.globalresearch.ca/the-cashless-society-is-almost-
here-and-with-some-very-sinister-implications/5313515

4.2 Economist Mike Kimball supports negative interest rates:
http://qz.com/21797/the-case-for-electric-money-the
-end-of-inflation-and-recessions-as-we-know-it/

4.3 Willem Buiter: https://willembuiter.com/

4.4 Link to Buiter's article: http://willembuiter.com/ELB.pdf

4.5 Ibid.

4.6 Bloomberg "Europe Dived Into Negative Rates and Now It Can't Find a Way Out" https://www.bloomberg.com/news/articles/2019-07-17/europe-dived-into-negative-rates-and-now-it-can-t-find-a-way-out

4.7 Riksbank exits negative interest rates in 2020: https://thedailycoin.org/2019/12/20/first-central-bank-exits-negative-interest-rates/

4.8 Kenneth Rogoff. 2014. Paper Money is Unfit for a World of High Crime and Low Inflation. http://scholar.harvard.edu/rogoff/publications/paper-money-unfit-world-high-crime-and-low-inflation

4.9 Schweizer Radio un Fernsehen (SRF) http://www.srf.ch/news/wirtschaft/negativzins-bank-verweigert-pensionskasse-bargeld-auszahlung

4.10 Heritage Foundation freedom ranking: http://www.heritage.org/index/ranking

4.11 Swiss banks refuse cash withdrawal to pension fund: https://mises.org/wire/swiss-bank-refuses-request-cash-withdrawal

4.12 Greek bank surcharge on cash withdrawals. http://www.dailymail.co.uk/news/article-3068975/Greece-introduces-mandatory-surcharges-cashpoints-desperate-attempt-raise-money-stop-panicked-citizens-withdrawing-life-savings-country-s-beleaguered-banks.html

Chapter 5

5.1 Future Role of Civil Society Report: http://www3.weforum.org/docs/WEF_FutureRoleCivilSociety_Report_2013.pdf

5.2 United Nations Capital Development Fund: https://www.uncdf.org/

5.3 Better Than Cash Alliance web site: http://betterthancash.org/

5.4 UNCDF definition of financial inclusion. https://www.
uncdf.org/financial-inclusion

5.5 Better Than Cash Alliance report: The Journey Toward
'Cash Lite.' https://www.betterthancash.org/tools-
research/reports/the-journey-toward-cash-lite
-addressing-poverty-saving-money-and-increasing
-transparency-by-accelerating-the-shift-to-electronic
-payments

5.6 The report references an article by authors Kumar and
Muhota (2012). Can Digital Footprints Lead to Greater
Financial Inclusion? Washington DC:CGAP (Consultative
Group to Assist the Poor) http://www.cgap.org/sites/
default/files/CGAP-Brief-Can-Digital-Footprints-Lead
-to-Greater-Financial-Inclusion-Jul-2012.pdf

5.7 Mastercard donates shares to its foundation: https://www.
fool.com/investing/general/2014/06/22/youll-never-
guess-who-owns-more-of-mastercard-than.aspx

5.8 Mastercard Foundation audited financial statements
12/31/2018: https://mastercardfdn.org/wp-content/
uploads/2019/07/1.-Mastercard-Foundation-Audited-FS
-as-of-December-31-2018.pdf

5.9 Mastercard Financial Inclusion Symposium panel video:
https://www.youtube.com/watch?v=qS1esNd1Qxk

5.10 G4S on inclusion/exclusion: https://www.g4s.com/
media-centre/news/2018/04/17/global-cash-report

5.11 Consultative Group to Assist the Poor:
http://www.cgap.org/

Chapter 6

6.1 Dave Birch: The Risk of Cashless Society Devolving into
an Electronic Somalia. Video. http://bankinnovation.
net/2015/02/the-risk-of-cashless-society-devolving-into
-an-electronic-somali-video/

6.2 Suds for Drugs. Tide detergent as currency. http://nymag.
com/news/features/tide-detergent-drugs-2013-1/

6.3 Honeybuns as currency in prisons. I originally found this story in the St. Petersburg Times, but they have deleted it from their website. A summary can be found here: https://gawker.com/5729214/honey-buns-are-the-new -prison-currency and a number of people found the story so interesting they appear to have posted the original Times article on various forums, such as https://www. tapatalk.com/groups/rpgaming/honey-buns-sweeten-life -for-florida-prisoners-t4843.html

6.4 Luna, JJ. Invisible Money, Hidden Assets, Secret Banking. 2013. http://www.amazon.com/ Invisible-Hidden-Assets-Secret-Accounts -ebook/dp/B00DF4SH0I/

Chapter 7

7.1 Buy gardening supplies, get raided by S.W.A.T. http://www.kctv5.com/story/23951053/ leawood-family-seeks-7-million-for-swat-style

7.2 Operation Choke Point explained in one minute on YouTube: https://youtu.be/7iaYPBk9i7M

7.3 Operation Choke Point and reform summary: https:// www.govtrack.us/congress/bills/115/hr2706/summary

7.4 The original list was reproduced here: https://www. cryptocoinsnews.com/dojs-operation-choke-point-driven -30-industries-bitcoin/ but that company was sold to CCN.com in 2017. The page with the list is no longer available. In fact, the list seems to have been scrubbed almost entirely from the web, with the exception of https://en.wikipedia.org/wiki/Operation_Choke_Point and in a letter from a Congressional Committee to the FDIC https://republicans-oversight.house.gov/wp -content/uploads/2014/06/2014-06-09-DEI-Jordan-to- Gruenberg-FDIC-Choke-Point-and-Reputational-Risk.pdf

7.5 Operation Chokepoint's rescinded list quotes: http://usconsumers.org/news/ fdic-letter-spell-end-operation-choke-point/

7.6 Congressional Oversight Committee on Operation Choke Point. https://republicans-oversight.house.gov/wp-content/uploads/2014/12/Staff-Report-FDIC-and-Operation-Choke-Point-12-8-2014.pdf

7.7 FDIC Retreats from Operation Choke Point: https://cei.org/blog/fdic-retreats-operation-choke-point

7.8 Bank closes topless dancer's account. http://www.americanbanker.com/gallery/timeline-operation-choke-point-1066360-1.html Author note: This web page still exists but the comments section where I got the quote has been eliminated as of March 2020.

7.9 Powderhorn Outfitters and Operation Choke Point. http://dailycaller.com/2014/05/31/gun-seller-dropped-by-bank-rejects-their-attempt-to-kiss-and-make-up/

7.10 Operation Choke Point attacks adult entertainers. https://www.techdirt.com/articles/20140430/12191027079/chase-bank-slutshaming-might-only-be-them-dancing-to-dojs-twisted-puppet-strings.shtml

https://news.vice.com/article/is-the-doj-forcing-banks-to-terminate-the-accounts-of-porn-stars

7.11 Michael's Pawn & Gun. http://dailysignal.com/2015/05/12/small-business-owner-says-bank-denied-service-because-she-sells-guns/

7.12 American Gun and Pawn: http://www.wfla.com/story/28655000/bank-closes-brooksville-pawn-gun-shop-owners-account [Note: this story appears to have been scrubbed from the WFLA website]

7.13 Suntrust statement: https://www.cfsponline.com/chokepoint/details.htm?ArticleID=31428

7.14 Congressmen agree, Choke Point involved: http://www.wfla.com/story/28834615/protest-at-brooksville-suntrust-draws-supporters-of-gun-and-pawn-shop

7.15 Griffin, G. Edward. The Creature from Jekyll Island. 5th Ed., September 2010. American Media. POB 4646, Westlake Village, CA 91359. Page 563.

7.16 SunTrust Bank $1 billion settlement: https://www. latimes.com/business/la-fi-suntrust-mortgage-settlement -20140618-story.html

7.17 Congressman requests information on Operation Choke Point. https://www.convenience.org/Archive/News/ NACSDailyArticles/2014/ND1117144

7.18 Frank Keating on Operation Choke Point: http://www. wsj.com/articles/SB10001424052702304810904579511911 684102106

7.19 H.R. 2706: https://www.govtrack.us/congress/bills/115/ hr2706

H.R. 189: https://www.govtrack.us/congress/bills/116/ hr189

7.20 Chase Bank account closings: https://www. theepochtimes.com/chase-bank-denies-political-motives -after-controversy-erupts-over-closed-accounts_ 2884333.html

7.21 Journalist and activist Lara Loomer blacklisted: https:// www.breitbart.com/tech/2019/02/06/paypal-blacklists -jewish-conservative-activist-laura-loomer/

7.22 Robert Spencer: https://www.jihadwatch.org/2018/08/ patreon-and-mastercard-ban-robert-spencer-without- explanation

7.23 PayPal cutting off "fringe" groups: https://www.foxnews. com/opinion/paypal-has-politically-weaponized-the- financial-system-by-aligning-with-hard-left

7.24 https://www.buzzfeednews.com/article/ blakemontgomery/the-alt-right-has-a-payment -processor-problem#.kvwGlPX2lQ

Chapter 9

9.1 CPI calculator online: http://www.bls.gov/data/inflation_ calculator.htm

9.2 CPI understates true inflation: http://www.shadowstats. com/alternate_data/inflation-charts

9.3 Boring, Perianne. Forbes. 2014: http://www.forbes.com/ sites/perianneboring/2014/02/03/if-you-want-to-know -the-real-rate-of-inflation-dont-bother-with-the-cpi/

9.4 Members of Congress Get Abnormally High Returns from Their Stocks: http://www.huffingtonpost. com/2011/05/24/members-of-congress-get-a_n_ 866387.html

Chapter 11

11.1 IRS Authority: http://www.irs.gov/irm/part9/irm_ 09-007-002.html

11.2 https://www.law.cornell.edu/uscode/text/21/881

11.3 The story of Matt Lee: http://reason.com/ blog/2014/09/10/final-chapter-of-cash-seizure-series-a-r

I originally encountered Matt's story in the form of a letter he had published in the online Silver Pinyon Journal. That web site no longer seems to be online, so I have linked to a summary of Matt's story on Reason.com. Many web sites have written about Matt's unfortunate experience.

11.4 U.S. vs. $133,420 in currency. http://cdn.ca9.uscourts. gov/datastore/opinions/2012/02/21/10-16727.pdf

11.5 U.S. Currency contaminated by cocaine. http:// www.snopes.com/business/money/cocaine. asp#Zjm8TfKlSG6sxq0i.99

11.6 Pittsburg Airport Forfeiture: https://ij.org/case/ pittsburgh-forfeiture/

11.7 DEA to return seized money: https://reason. com/2020/03/04/dea-returns-82k-life-savings-it-seized -from-an-elderly-pittsburgh-man-and-his-daughter/

11.8 $4 billion in cash seizures: https://oig.justice.gov/ reports/2017/e1702.pdf

11.9 Cash seizure at Tampa Airport: https://www.fox9.com/ news/government-agents-seized-181500-in-cash-at -airport-and-wont-give-it-back

11.10 John Oliver explains civil asset forfeiture. [Video: 16:29 mins] https://youtu.be/3kEpZWGgJks

Chapter 12

12.1 U.S. v. U.S. Currency, $30,060: http://openjurist.org/39/f3d/1039

12.2 Rodriguez v. United States 741 F. 3d 905: https://www.law.cornell.edu/supremecourt/text/13-9972

Chapter 13

13.1 Someone Must Be Telling Lies: http://takimag.com/article/someone_must_be_telling_lies_theodore_dalrymple

Dr. Daniels publishes fine articles at http://www.skepticaldoctor.com

13.2 Banking Secrecy Act Manual: https://bsaaml.ffiec.gov/manual/RegulatoryRequirements/05

13.3 Banks told to monitor your transactions: https://www.fincen.gov/sites/default/files/shared/FIN-2012-G001.pdf

13.4 US, SunTrust Announce Nearly $1B Settlement. SunTrust Bank $1 billion settlement: https://www.latimes.com/business/la-fi-suntrust-mortgage-settlement-20140618-story.html

13.5 5 Banks Plead Guilty: http://www.nytimes.com/2015/05/21/business/dealbook/5-big-banks-to-pay-billions-and-plead-guilty-in-currency-and-interest-rate-cases.html

13.6 HSBC Helped Terrorists, Iran, Mexican Drug Cartels Launder Money: http://www.forbes.com/sites/afontevecchia/2012/07/16/hsbc-helped-terrorists-iran-mexican-drug-cartels-launder-money-senate-report-says/

Chapter 14

14.1 FinCEN Notice to Customers: http://www.fincen.gov/whatsnew/pdf/CTRPamphletBW.pdf

14.2 Why people innocently engage in illegal structuring activities: https://www.washingtonpost.com/news/wonk/wp/2017/04/05/the-irs-took-millions-from-innocent-people-because-of-how-they-managed-their-bank-accounts-inspector-general-finds/

14.3 IRS seizes Carol Hinders' bank account: http://www.desmoinesregister.com/story/news/investigations/2015/04/04/forfeiture-mrs-ladys-carole-hinders/25309217/

14.4 IRS agrees to return Hinders' money: http://www.businessinsider.com/the-irs-agrees-to-return-carole-hinders-money-2014-12

14.5 Bi-County Distributors seizure: http://www.bizjournals.com/bizjournals/washingtonbureau/2015/02/irs-seizes-millions-from-law-abiding-businesses-3.html?page=all

14.6 South Mountain Creamery seizure: http://www.washingtonpost.com/local/dc-politics/uncle-sam-may-have-picked-the-wrong-cash-cow/2015/04/14/227aa73c-de2e-11e4-a500-1c5bb1d8ff6a_story.html

14.7 Clyde Armory seizure: http://onlineathens.com/local-news/2015-02-12/athens-gun-shop-owner-testifies-congress-asset-seizure

14.8 IRS announcement of new policy: http://www.nytimes.com/2014/10/26/us/statement-of-richard-weber-chief-of-irs-criminal-investigation.html?_r=0

14.9 Policy Directive 15-3: http://www.justice.gov/sites/default/files/opa/press-releases/attachments/2015/03/31/ag-memo-structuring-policy-directive.pdf

14.10 Janet Malone seizure: http://www.desmoinesregister.com/story/news/2015/02/10/dubuque-widow-hubands-cash-deposits-lawsuit/23195305/

14.11 Janet Malone sentenced: https://www.desmoinesregister.com/story/news/crime-and-courts/2015/05/13/judge-orders-fine-iowa-widow-split-up-bank-deposits/27250015/

14.12 L & M Convenience Mart: http://dailysignal.com/2015/05/11/the-irs-seized-107000-from-this-north-carolina-mans-bank-account-now-hes-fighting-to-get-it-back/

14.13 Justice Dept. not following its own policy. [Video. 1:20 min]: https://youtu.be/16aYGRoswWw

14.14 Institute for Justice is helping McLelland: http://dailysignal.com/2015/05/14/federal-government-to-return-107702-irs-seized-from-north-carolina-convenience-store-owner/

14.15 Government returning money: https://www.dailysignal.com/2015/05/14/federal-government-to-return-107702-irs-seized-from-north-carolina-convenience-store-owner/

14.16 Loopholes in Justice Department's new policy: http://www.washingtonpost.com/blogs/federal-eye/wp/2015/03/31/holder-announces-new-limits-on-civil-asset-forfeitures/

14.17 Institute for Justice report. Seize First, Question Later. February 2015:https://www.ij.org/?s=seize+first+question+later

14.18 Taxpayer First Act signed by Trump: https://ij.org/press-release/trump-signs-bill-to-protects-small-business-owners-from-irs-seizures/

14.19 Ibid

Chapter 15

15.1 Harry Reid on our "voluntary" tax system. [Video. 4:11 min]: https://youtu.be/H6q0slMhDw8

15.2 Text of the 16th Amendment to the U.S. Constitution: https://www.law.cornell.edu/constitution/amendmentxvi

15.3 Internal Revenue Code section 61(a): https://www.law.cornell.edu/uscode/text/26/61

15.4 Title 26, Part III: https://www.law.cornell.edu/uscode/text/26/subtitle-A/chapter-1/subchapter-B/part-III

15.5 Internal Revenue Code section 1: https://www.law
.cornell.edu/uscode/text/26/1

15.6 Internal Revenue Code section 63: https://www.law
.cornell.edu/uscode/text/26/63

15.7 Brief history of the withholding tax: http://www.
independent.org/newsroom/article.asp?id=2092

This tax was put in place to collect money to fund World
War II. As a side benefit that did not go unnoticed,
automatic withholding made the withholding practically
invisible to workers. Before, they had to actually write a
check to the government each quarter.

15.8 IRS audit techniques for small business and self
-employed: https://www.irs.gov/businesses/small
-businesses-self-employed/cash-intensive
-businesses-audit-techniques-guide-table-of-contents

Chapter 16

16.1 IRS audit techniques for small business and self
-employed: https://www.irs.gov/businesses/small
-businesses-self-employed/cash-intensive
-businesses-audit-techniques-guide-table-of-contents

Chapter 17

17.1 Office of Inspector General FDIC's Implementation of
the PATRIOT Act: https://www.fdicoig.gov/sites/default/
files/publications/03-037.pdf

17.2 Businesses classified as financial institutions by the
Patriot Act: https://www.law.cornell.edu/uscode/
text/31/5312

17.3 https://www.m-s-lawyers.com/about-us/colorado
-attorney-publications/patriot-act-impacts-small
-businesses.html

17.4 Specially Designated Nationals List: http://www.treas
.gov/offices/enforcement/ofac/sdn/index.html

Chapter 18

18.1 Fourth Industrial Revolution: https://www.weforum.org/
agenda/2016/01/the-fourth-industrial-revolution-what-it
-means-and-how-to-respond/

18.2 Fourth Industrial Revolution defined: https://www.
researchgate.net/publication/323638914_The_Fourth_
Industrial_Revolution_Opportunities_and_Challenges

Chapter 19

19.1 Massachusetts cash acceptance law: https://www.
bostonmagazine.com/news/2018/02/06/cashless-boston/

19.2 Philadelphia bans cash free stores: https://www.npr.
org/2019/03/08/701076862/protecting-the-unbanked-by
-banning-cashless-businesses-in-philadelphia

19.3 New York City and other locations ban cashless
businesses: https://www.npr.org/2020/02/06/803003343/
some-businesses-are-going-cashless-but-cities-are-
pushing-back

19.4 GS4 Global Cash Report: https://www.g4s.com/news
-and-insights/insights/2018/04/17/g4s-world-cash-report
-reveals-global-cash-payments-are-on-the-increase

19.5 ECB supports proposed cash access law in Sweden:
https://cashessentials.org/ecb-welcomes-swedish-draft
-law-ordering-banks-to-provide-cash-services/

19.6 ECB published opinion: https://www.ecb.europa.eu/ecb/
legal/pdf/en_con_2019_41_f_sign.pdf

Chapter 20

20.1 Thomas E. Woods podcast #348: http://tomwoods.com/
podcast/ep-348-the-dui-racket-revisited/

Chapter 21

21.1 Choosing to be Unbanked. Thomas W. Miller,
Jr.: http://mercatus.org/expert_commentary/
choosing-be-unbanked

21.2 Daisy Luther on deliberate "unbanking":
http://www.theorganicprepper.ca/
how-to-break-up-with-your-bank-03242013

Chapter 22

22.1 American Express survey: http://www.cnbc.com/
id/102377632

Chapter 23

23.1 Carson, Dale C. Arrest Proof Yourself. 2007. Page 244.

23.2 Don't Talk to the Police. [Video. 46.38 min]: https://
youtu.be/d-7o9xYp7eE. I highly recommend that
everyone in your family and all of your friends watch
this video.

23.3 Carson, Dale C. Arrest Proof Yourself. 2007. Page 231.

23.4 Luna, JJ. Invisible Money, Hidden Assets, Secret
Accounts: http://www.amazon.com/Invisible
-Hidden-Assets-Secret-Accounts-ebook/dp/
B00DF4SH0I/

Chapter 24

24.1 Murray, Charles. By the People: Rebuilding Liberty
Without Permission. 2015: http://www.amazon.com/
People-Rebuilding-Liberty-Without-Permission-ebook/
dp/B00N6PBGM2/

24.2 Alibaba app in China: https://thenextweb.com/
china/2020/03/03/chinas-covid-19-app-reportedly-color
-codes-people-and-shares-data-with-cops/

24.3 Locate X software: https://www.protocol.com/
government-buying-location-data?

Discover Even More Ways to _Save_ Money Every Month!

The Franklin Prosperity Report is dedicated to helping its readers save money each month with creative ways to cut your costs on groceries, insurance, travel, and everyday expenses so you can save more and spend less this year. Named after one of our Founding Fathers, **Benjamin Franklin**, the newsletter follows Franklin's centuries-old wisdom and his principles of building wealth. After all, it was Franklin who said "A Penny Saved Is a Penny Earned," and it is the motto we have adopted for the newsletter.

Each month _The Franklin Prosperity Report_ follows in its namesake's footsteps and gives readers invaluable advice from a host of top-shelf, expert contributors on how to properly manage and maximize your money. Recent issues have included topics such as:

- Cut Your Tax Bill in Retirement! 6 Proven Financial Strategies to Keep More of Your Hard-Earned Cash

- Stop Overpaying for Health Insurance! 8 Ways to Put Your Money to Work for You in a Health Savings Account

- Baby Boomer Guide to a Fully Funded Retirement

If you would like to learn more about joining _The Franklin Prosperity Report_ and how it can help you keep more money in your pocket each month, go to:

WWW.NEWSMAX.COM/CASH

My RETIREMENT *Date*

How would you like to know the exact date you can expect to retire? Well, this **FREE** assessment will help you learn exactly that. And more importantly, we give you some fun tools that you can use so you'll retire quicker, safer, and wealthier than you ever imagined . . . along with simple investment strategies to help ensure you NEVER run out of money during your retirement. Enjoy!

Find out *your* retirement date!

Go To:

MyRetirementDate.com/Cash

Powered by NewsmaxFinance.com